D1570877

Rule #1: STOP TALKING!

A GUIDE TO LISTENING

Linda Eve Diamond

Listeners Press

Published by Listeners Press
a division of Happy About®

First Printing: November, 2007
Paperback ISBN: 1600050670 (978-1-60005-067-1)
Place of Publication: Silicon Valley, California, USA
Paperback Library of Congress Number: 2007938429
eBook ISBN: 1600050689 (978-1-60005-068-8)

———— **Praise for** ————

RULE #1: STOP TALKING
A Guide to Listening

"*RULE #1: STOP TALKING!* is an excellent introduction to Listening as a powerful communication tool. Linda translates, through listening, the
principles of human understanding into the concerns of our everyday lives and encourages readers to begin their own listening journeys and to
explore the effects of good listening."

**~ Dr. Margarete Imhof, President, International
Listening Association (ILA)**

"In a world rushing by and filled with so much
noise, nobody seems to be listening. Linda Eve
Diamond has brought forth a book that opens a
door to deep listening, something simple yet
powerful to improve relationships, work and
well-being. Good lessons and important tools in
a busy life."

**~ Stephan Rechtschaffen, MD, Co-Founder,
Omega Holistic Institute**

"With her bright, friendly tone, and practical, commonsensical approach, Diamond eases you into something that's bigger than you may realize. To truly listen is to break free from the limitations of your own concepts and expectations and open to limitless fresh possibilities. Step by step, *Rule #1* shows you how."

~ Dean Sluyter, author of *Cinema Nirvana: Enlightenment Lessons from the Movies*

"Linda writes in a voice that makes it easy for people to understand the basic concepts of listening. In addition, she adds the practical information about physiology and biology—how it works! I also like her definitions and the techniques she suggests. I think readers will come away with a lot of ideas on how to become better listeners."

~ Kay Lindahl, founder of The Listening Center, Long Beach, California

"Diamond's book deserves a good listening to. Human beings are human becomings—works in progress—and *Rule #1: Stop Talking* is a guide book to becoming more in tune with ourselves and one another."

~ Ronald Bell, Chief Evocateur Officer/Owner, Center for Positive Integral Change

ACKNOWLEDGEMENTS

I would first like to thank Mitchell Levy,
my publisher, for listening, believing, and
creating the *Listeners Press* division.

My deep gratitude goes to the *listeners*
who speak in these pages, sharing their thoughts
and stories. This book is richer for their
insights, humor and wisdom:

William Carter
Billy Collins
Phyllis Dutwin
Jodi Gast
Natalie Gast
Laura Janusik
Emily Krestow, PhD
Walter Ladden
Kay Lindahl
Maria F. Loffredo Roca, PhD
Sandy Newman
Lisa M. Orick-Martinez, PhD
Michael Purdy, PhD
George Rozelle, PhD
Erin Tobiasz

Many thanks also to Ray Villarosa and
John Kissee for their artistic contributions.

This book is dedicated to
Michael and Harriet Diamond
and to *all* compassionate listeners who make
the words *friends* & *family* interchangeable.

Rule #1: STOP TALKING!
TABLE OF CONTENTS

INTRODUCTION

Rule #1: Stop Talking offers a light-hearted look at the serious subject of listening. While working on this book, I have been met by overwhelmingly enthusiastic responses. Sometimes I hear an eager, "I need that! When is it coming out?" Or, the second-most popular response: "I need to give that as a gift to my co-workers/boss/employees/friends/sister/husband/wife— *When can I get it?"*

Rule #1 is for everyone who wants to improve listening skills, for those who feel surrounded by people who need to, and for those to whom this book may be tactfully recommended. *Rule #1* addresses listening skills, speaking in a way that might encourage others to listen, and listening to yourself in terms of both how you sound to others *and* your own intuition.

Not listening at home causes misunderstandings and resentments. At work, add to that lost business and lost opportunities. Listening is the basis for all of the strong, enriching relationships in our lives.

Listening is an adventure into the worlds of those around us. It broadens us, lays the groundwork for peace, elevates the quality of our relationships, and opens the way for success. If nothing else, when you listen, you'll find you are the most popular person in the room. We all have listening skills and challenges. As I worked on this book, many people shared their wisdom, follies, and fun listening stories with me and allowed me to present them here in boxes titled, "Listeners Speak."

The remainder of this introduction, following the *Book Map,* is an optional *Listening Warmup.* Listening is something many of us don't think about very often. We do it—and don't do it—in a more or less automatic way. As you read *Rule #1,* you'll be putting a lot of focus on your listening "muscle," so the warm-up offers an opportunity to stretch it out, thinking about a few of your current listening skills and challenges. Because change is usually gradual, it is also helpful to have some idea of your starting point—or listening baseline—then check back in a few months to see how far you've come. The first is a *Self Assessment* and the second, *A Question of Perception,* provides an opportunity to see how others perceive your listening skills.

BOOK MAP

Chapter 1: *Listening 101,* provides a basic overview of the importance of listening which is, in essence, the placing of attention. Once you graduate from the *Listening 101* chapter, you will find some *Rules of Listening,* beginning with the most basic: *stop talk - ing,* then progressing through some that may be less obvious or more easily forgotten when we don't stop to think about them. The chapters on *Short Circuits* examine beliefs that interfere with—or "short circuit"—listening.

The chapter titled *TalkTalkTalk* takes a playful look at people who talk without pause or concern for others in the room. Why do they do it? Can they be stopped? How can one escape? The chapter also offers some practical solutions. After all that talk, you will find a chapter titled, *Nobody Listens to Me,* which is about how to encourage others to listen to *you.*

The book then delves into specific listening skills, such as *Lie Detection, Self Awareness, Conflict Resolution, Listening in the Age of Overload* and then clearing *Head Static* (such as the racing mind or repetitive thoughts). Here, the book touches on meditation, nutrition, and sleep, all of which keep the mind in a better state for focus and attention. The last chapter, *The Touchy-Feely Section* delves lightly into the deep human need for connection and reiterates the importance and impact of listening.

LISTENING WARM-UP

This warm-up section offers a starting point for listening self reflection, a benchmark for looking back, and a way to examine your listening skills in light of how they are perceived by others. Each is offered in both long and short forms, so consider completing whichever one works best for you. However, if quizzes make you queasy, please feel free to move ahead! *Consider and revisit your assessment answers as you read.*

Assessments

The Self Assessment that follows is a brief look at where you place your attention when interacting with others. (Answers may be quite different for work and home; you might choose to give separate answers for each.)

Questions of Perception is a chance to find out how others would rate your listening skills. *Give this to people in your life to answer and ask for their honest opinions.* Many of the questions mirror the ones in the *Self Assessment,* so this is your chance to see if the perceptions of others match your own. No one person's perception equals reality, but learn how your listening skills are perceived—and be open to thinking about whether someone has a good point.

Self Assessment

Yes/No

_____ 1. I like to multi-task and think about other things when people are talking.

_____ 2. If people aren't going to take my advice, they shouldn't waste my time telling me their problems.

_____ 3. I'm usually bored when the conversation doesn't center around my interests.

_____ 4. When someone is slow to get a point across, I interrupt to get things moving.

_____ 5. When people speak to me, they most often have to compete with a number of distractions.

_____ 6. I tend to be involved in a lot of misunderstandings.

_____ 7. A person's appearance, grammar, or style of speaking affect how much attention I give them.

_____ 8. I have trouble keeping a confidence.

_____ 9. I usually feel that making my case is more important that someone else's feelings.

_____ 10. When I don't understand something, I will often fake it and smile instead of asking questions.

_____ 11. I'm good at looking like I'm listening when I'm not. Most people don't notice.

_____ 12. I tend to talk when I should be listening.

_____ 13. I trust my intuition and it serves me well.

_____ 14. I can usually tell when people aren't being honest with me.

_____ 15. I am good at soothing conflict situations and finding win-win solutions.

Assessing Your Self Assessment

A *perfect score* would be *No* to questions 1-12 and *Yes* to 13-15. If you answered *Yes* for any number from 1-12, look at these as areas you might want to strengthen. As you place your attention on those areas and make small shifts, notice any subtle changes in your work or home relationships. If you answered *No* to most of them and *Yes* to questions 13-15, you have some solid listening foundations. If your answers show areas that you wish to improve, not to worry. You have already begun the process by assessing where you are now and will continue to strengthen these skills as you continue to read and place your attention on listening.

Mini Self Assessment

This mini-assessment is the short version for those who prefer a quicker quiz. It may also be used in addition to the *Self Assessment* and is equally useful for warming up listening and for looking back, over time.

Ask yourself:

1. What are my listening strengths?

2. What are my listening challenges?

3. How will improving my listening skills improve my personal and/or business relationships?

4. Do I listen to my own intuition? When I have, has it guided me well?

Questions of Perception

Yes/No   Does this "listener"...

_____   1.   often multi-task or seem distracted when you are talking?

_____   2.   become annoyed when you don't take his/her advice?

_____   3.   seem bored when the conversation doesn't center around his/her interests?

_____   4.   frequently interrupt?

_____   5.   allow interruptions or distractions (such as taking calls) when you wish he/she wouldn't?

_____   6.   seem to be involved in a lot of misunderstandings (with you and/or others)?

_____   7.   seem to allow a speaker's appearance, grammar or style of speaking to affect how much attention he/she will give that person?

_____   8.   show that he/she can be trusted to keep a confidence?

_____   9.   bulldoze over others' feelings to make a point?

_____   10.   show genuine interest and ask questions when discussing issues that are complex or especially important to you?

_____   11.   ever seem to be *pretending* to listen?

_____   12.   seem impatient and quick to draw conclusions?

_____   13.   tend to talk when he/she should be listening?

Reviewing Questions of Perception

A perfect score would be *Yes* to questions 8 and 10 and *No* to all others. Review all answers carefully and ask follow-up questions. Compare answers with your own self assessment and consider areas that do not match. You might learn things about how others perceive you that are encouraging, and you might learn of areas you need to strengthen, or even that people notice more than you think they do. *Make notes on the feedback you receive and check back with the same people as you progress on your listening journey. They do not need to revisit the entire assessment, but ask about those questions that were areas of concern.*

Mini Questions of Perception Assessment

It may be difficult to have certain people fill out a 12 question assessment. For them, you can offer a quick mini-assessment. These questions would also be helpful to discuss with those who take your *Questions of Perception* assessment.

Ask your friends/family/coworkers:

1. Do you consider me a good listener? Why/Why not?

2. Can you tell me about a time when you felt I wasn't listening? What did you need from me that you didn't get (emotional support, empathy, an action, a reaction, advice, etc.)?

CHAPTER 1

LISTENING 101

"What people really need
is a good listening to."

Mary Lou Casey

~ 1 ~

LEARNING TO LISTEN

We learned how to speak; we learned the 3 r's: reading, writing and 'rithmetic. We were told *to* listen, but most of us were never instructed on the finer points of listening, and the closest anyone got to specifics was that we should be quiet.

When we wanted to listen to lectures but couldn't tame our minds; when we encountered misunderstandings; when we felt alone, or lacked concentration, most of us had no course available called Listening 101. In a good Listening 101 course, we would have been taught to evaluate sources, raise questions, and think critically. We also would have learned why listening is not as simple as it seems and how to evaluate and work with our own listening challenges.

Back to basics—on the first day of Listening 101, our instructor would have pointed out that listening is often wrongly equated with hearing.

LISTENING VS. HEARING

Most of us with adequate hearing think we're born listeners just because our ears work. That's like saying you are a born pianist because your family had a piano in the house. But just as people with hearing loss can be thoughtful, attentive listeners, not all people with perfect hearing *are* attentive listeners.

Here's the basic hearing action: sound waves enter the auditory canal and find their way, via impulses to the brain. In other words, hearing happens. Listening is usually more a matter of choice. So, we have all had the experience of overhearing or being part of a scenario like this one: Someone implies the "listener" is not listening, and the "listener" snaps: "I heard you!" To be fair, the person *did hear*, but we all know that's not the same as listening. Maybe that person was listening and maybe not. But some common follow-up phrases to, *"I heard you!"* are "You never told me that!" "Oops—is that what you were saying?" or "I didn't hear you."

It's not wrong, in the English language, to use listening and hearing interchangeably: "Did you hear what she said?" "I can't hear you when you're shouting." However, that usage may signal a shortcoming in the language that requires us to be somewhat more vigilant about meaning. When we say we heard someone, genuinely believing that we somehow processed information simply because we heard the sounds of a familiar voice in the background of a game, a TV show, or Web surfing, we need to ask ourselves whether we *listened*.

LISTENING DEFINED

The International Listening Association (ILA), an organization dedicated to the study, development, and teaching of effective listening, defines listening as "the process of receiving, constructing meaning from, and responding to spoken and/or non-verbal messages." It's no mistake that this definition of listening encompasses non-verbal messages. Listening is so much broader than our auditory canals.

Listening is paying attention, creating a space for the speaker's ideas, and being present. Harville Hendrix, author and relationship guru, coined the use of the word *presence* as a verb, *to presence*. He refers to listening as *presencing*, defined as "the non-judgmental placement of attention."

One way to hone the skill of listening, that placing of attention, is to enter into listening in touch with your own genuine *interest* or *empathy*.

Interest: None of us knows everything, so all of us have something to learn, and a general sense of interest in learning is a strong basis for effective listening. Even if you're in a lecture or a meeting that seems particularly boring, listen for that needle in the haystack that's interesting so you can walk away and say, "Well, at least I got this nifty needle." The key is not to go in expecting your time to be wasted; expect that you might actually learn something.

If you have no interest whatsoever in a particular topic, but you have to learn it, use some of the listening techniques offered throughout this book to keep you focused. You are there for a reason. If you can't tap into any level of interest in the topic, ask yourself why you're there—it may be that you're in the wrong place. If you're in the right place, you're there for a reason. Try giving in and listening. It usually passes the time more quickly than not listening, and you'll have the added bonus of learning something.

Empathy: Also at the heart of listening is *heart*, and empathy helps us listen. Put yourself in the speaker's place. If you can feel for someone, you'll be more open to taking in the message. Sure, there are times when you're taking in dry information that has almost no human component, but in many listening situations it helps to understand the speaker's perspective. Becoming a better listener requires us to delve more deeply into what it means to place our attention.

THE POWER OF THE LISTENER

We tend to think of speakers as leaders and listeners as followers, but listening is not a passive activity; the listener is always learning. Also, people tend to gravitate to listeners. People who are great speakers but lousy listeners can be fun to have around, but a good listener makes us feel more comfortable and, often, more valued.

Have you ever noticed how the listener affects your energy, comfort, enthusiasm, or nervousness as you speak? Have you ever felt your own enthusiasm waning when you shared something exciting with someone who seemed uninterested or preoccupied? What happens if you share news with someone who's thrilled for you? Does the excitement build? What about bad news, bad moods, or nervousness? If you're agitated and you speak to someone who seems to be uninterested or not paying attention, you're likely to become more agitated, whereas speaking to someone who is focused and interested can help to relax you. Have you ever felt more accustomed to *not* being listened to than being listened to? How does it feel, then, when someone actually listens?

BENEFITS TO THE SPEAKER

Obviously, being listened to allows the speaker to make a point; it can also reduce the speaker's anxiety, help the speaker maintain flow and clarity, and, depending upon the circumstance, can even be an antidepressant. It can't always solve the problem, but the act of expressing oneself and being listened to without judgment is often healing, encouraging or inspiring.

On the other hand, if someone is speaking and the listener is reading mail, web surfing, or somehow not paying attention, the speaker will easily feel disempowered. You might have had the experience of having someone not listening to you when it was important for you to express yourself. *Expression* may implode and become *depression* when someone who needs to be heard speaks and no one is listening.

BENEFITS TO THE LISTENER

Listening not only benefits the speaker, but also the listener. The simple act of listening may contribute to:

- **Improved memory:** The act of focused attention aids in retention.
- **Broader knowledge base:** Listening is a pathway to learning.
- **Healthier relationships:** Others feel more respected and understood.

- **Greater productivity:** Listening prevents time spent working on the wrong thing *and* people thrive, feeling more confident and appreciated, when listened to.

- **Saved time from fewer misunderstandings:** Listening reduces misunderstandings, which often cost time and money.

- **Improved self confidence:** Gaining a greater understanding of others (and ourselves) increases confidence.

- **Strength in negotiations:** Listening reveals subtle clues and helps us find win-win solutions.

- **Greater health, happiness, and well being for people we care about:** Well being improves when we feel listened to and respected.

- **Increased sense of empowerment and confidence in those around us:** Listening encourages and supports others, giving them the strength and freedom to draw their own conclusions.

- **More "aha" moments:** Insights come from unlikely sources when we're listening.

- **Strong relationships:** Listening strengthens relationships—business and personal.

- **Success:** Listening helps save time, analyze needs, and communicate for greater success.

- **Health:** *Not* listening can lead to misunderstandings, arguments, and stress.

- **Increased blood and oxygen to the brain:** Listening has been documented to have some of the same effects as meditation.

Listeners Speak

Enter the Other's World

True listening is not passive. More than 30 years as a psychoanalyst has taught me that real listening is a highly active process.

As an active listener, I am allowed entrance into another person's life story. A privilege. It is not about me. It is not my life story. I learn to see the world through the other person's eyes by asking questions and questioning my own assumptions. This allows me to experience an event not as I would experience it in my world, but as it would be experienced in the other's world. For example, if I stay solely in my world, I might not be upset at all if what happened to someone else happened to me. I might then say to the other, "It is not so bad," or "Time will help," or, "It could be worse." Thus, we try to be helpful. But we only succeed in increasing the speaker's pain and feelings of being misunderstood.

How are the outside world's intimate relationships different from what I do in my office? It is true that therapist and patient are both listening to each other, but all intimate relationships involve two people who both need to listen to the other in the same way, with each trying to enter the other person's world as he or she experiences it. Let's say you are unhappy with someone you love for some reason. That person must be able to understand why you are unhappy, not to necessarily accept your view as factual, but to know why it is true for you. Only then can that unhappiness be let go.

Emily Krestow, PhD
Psychoanalyst
Hollywood, FL ~ www.EmilyKrestow.com

LISTENING AND HEALTH

Believe it or not, listening *is* good for health. When we listen attentively, heart rate and oxygen consumption are reduced; blood pressure decreases. Interestingly, deep listening has some of the same effects on the body as deep meditation.

Dr. Dean Ornish, author of *Dr. Dean Ornish's Program for Reversing Heart Disease; The Only System Scientifically Proven to Reverse Heart Disease Without Drugs or Surgery*, advocates listening as part of a healthy and healing lifestyle. In describing his program, he says that while he advocates a healthy diet and exercise, deeper levels must also be addressed: "...Teaching people how to quiet down the mind and to gain more control over it; how to listen to others' feelings and to their own; how to feel more connected to others and to themselves; how to give and receive love more fully."

LISTENING AND MEMORY

Memory is a vast, complex subject that expands far beyond the scope of listening; however, listening is a great place to start. Often, we think we're losing our memories when it's only a case of scattered attention.

Do you want to keep your brain active and fight off memory loss as you age? Researchers recommend exercising our brains, and a simple form of exercise is listening. Positron emission tomography PET scans (designed to see blood flow to and through the brain) have shown increased flow when the brain is focused on an activity (such as paying focused attention). Researcher Alan Lockwood set out to show the difference in brain activity when someone is only passively hearing sounds vs. listening attentively. Scans taken as participants listened showed increased blood flow and involvement of more brain regions compared to participants who were subjected to random sounds that involved hearing more than listening.

But going back to basics, memory is a three-step process:

encode, store, and retrieve. If you're not focused on listening, the information cannot be encoded. If your mind is busy making judgments about the speaker, making plans for tomorrow, thinking, "I'll never remember this," it's hard to encode the information. Also, as you may imagine, "Yeah, whatever" is not the sound of information being encoded. Listening can improve memory by putting your brain to work and by creating the kind of focus that brings information from short-term to long-term memory. There is more to memory, but listening is a good start.

THE BUSINESS END OF LISTENING

Listening is essential for business success. Not listening causes misunderstandings and mistakes, which, in turn, cause lost time, lost money, and wasted resources; not listening creates a lack of trust, which affects motivation, productivity, and morale; and not listening can lead to a total communication breakdown. In short, not listening to clients, customers, patients, suppliers, employees, employers, or contractors is deadly for business.

Listening is key to customer retention, referrals and overall positive customer experiences. Unless you've developed the cure for the common cold, odds are people can go elsewhere. Customer service surveys continually find that most customers stay with a company for the service. Price, quality, and technical skills are factors, but service is king, and listening is at the heart of service.

Those businesses with foundations built on listening are the ones that come up with creative insights, products, and ways to move ahead. Innovation comes from *listening* to demand. Do you know what your customers really want? What about customer retention and referrals? You learn what makes people happy, what makes them feel valued, and what makes them feel they're getting value from you by *listening*. Listening also earns you the highly-respected reputation for caring. That raises your stock with customers or clients, employees, suppliers, and partners—*anyone* who comes in contact with your company.

THE BASIC STORYBOARD OF LISTENING

Where do we go wrong with listening? Listening includes four stages: hearing, interpreting, evaluating, and responding. Listening glitches occur at any stage.

Stage 1: Hearing is the first step on the basic storyboard. (Although listening is not solely an auditory experience, hearing is usually the first step to taking in and processing messages.)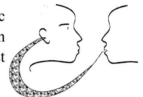

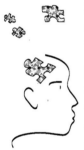 **Stage 2: Interpretation** can be tricky because it is automatic, based on perceptions and past experience. Though it is possible to slow down and take stock of our perceptions, we have to first acknowledge that our interpretation is not necessarily a universal truth. How we take in information can have nearly as much to do with what's already in our heads as it has to do with the information presented.

Stage 3: Evaluation is another potentially tricky stage. What do you make of what you hear? What will you do with this information? How do you fit it into your perceptions? Are you shifting information to make it fit? This is also where your brain determines whether information is of passing interest or should be incorporated into long-term memory.

Stage 4: Response seems like such a natural reaction that it ought to go unsaid. How can this be a step someone would skip? It happens. Someone fails to respond at all or, instead of responding, throws out a totally unrelated thought. Response is the last part of the listening process, but to the speaker who wants to feel understood, it's as important as the first.

A FEW FACTS ABOUT HEARING

In most cases, if someone hasn't listened, the glitch was in the interpretation or evaluation stage. Sometimes, though, listening gaffs *are* caused by hearing problems. Much frustration comes from people not realizing they have hearing problems, or ignoring them. So, before we delve into the deeper stages of listening, it might help to think about a basic equipment check and, for those with adequate hearing, the importance of hearing maintenance. Most of us take working equipment for granted. We also tend to make two assumptions: first, that our ears are designed for whatever decibel we can blast at them; and second, that significant hearing loss as we age is inevitable. Neither is true.

We've amplified sound beyond what the body's natural defenses are geared to handle, and there is evidence that when hearing fades away with age, it's more a case of noise-induced hearing loss having taken a toll over time than a simple case of the ears getting old and tired. In our society, we regularly accept high-level insults to the ears. According to a study by Dr. Samuel Rosen, a New York specialist, the average sixty-year-old in Africa hears as well or better than the average twenty-five year old in North America. Your ears aren't getting old. They've probably just had too much stress, drugs, and rock and roll. (I mean *no* disrespect to rock and roll—this refers to *any* excessively loud music or sounds.)

STRESS, DRUGS, AND ROCK AND ROLL

Stress: Believe it or not, prolonged stress can affect your hearing as much as other aspects of health. Cells need an adequate supply of nutrients and oxygen carried to them by the blood. Stress causes vessels to constrict, which reduces the amount of blood that can flow through them. The tiny capillaries that supply hair cells in the inner ear are especially sensitive to stress. Stress reduction is good for every cell in your body.

Drugs: Obviously, any mind-altering drug affects listening and focus skills as well as overall health. Surprisingly, though, certain pharmaceuticals can cause hearing loss. These are called "ototoxic" drugs. Neil Bauman, PhD, claimed years ago to have identified 550 drugs that could damage hearing. As Dr. Bauman explained, "If everyone who took a drug woke up deaf, there would be a huge outcry. However, when the damage is not readily apparent and may take months or years before we notice anything wrong, no one says anything. These resulting hearing losses are put down to 'normal' aging." Do what is necessary if you need these drugs, but it's always helpful to be aware of potential side effects.

Decibels: And the #1 most common cause of hearing loss... *no drum roll, please:* loud noises. The Occupational Safety & Health Administration (OSHA) is responsible for seeing that employees are protected from dangerously high decibels levels (providing ear protectors and safety information when workers are exposed to extended periods of 85 decibels or higher) but they can't keep up with nightclubs. The music in many clubs ranges from 85-100 decibels. A survey done in California by *The Bay Area Reporter* found that the loudest club in San Francisco blasted music up to 115 decibels, louder than a sand blaster or jackhammer. The Royal National Institute for Deaf People (RNID), a charity representing the nine million deaf and hard of hearing people in the UK, found that 62% of regular club goers have symptoms of hearing loss. According to RNID's former Chief Executive James Strachan, "We are roller-coasting towards an epidemic of hearing loss in middle rather than older age." In fact, the prevalence of hearing loss is increasing in younger ages, too.

If you love loud dance clubs, *practice safe sax* and use protection; you'll still hear the music and feel the sound pulsing through you if you wear earplugs and avoid standing next to the speakers.

Headphone users should be especially aware of decibels. Again, unsafe use of these devices causes gradual loss that won't be noticed until the damage is done. They can be used without injury if hearing safety guidelines are followed.

According to American Speech-Learning-Hearing Association (ASHA) Past President Alex Johnson: "We know first-hand that there are people who are listening at 110 to 120 decibels—a level equal, in terms of potential damage, to plugging the sound of a chain saw into one's ears." Johnson goes on to point out that chain saw operators wear *earplugs*.

Many portable music players offer volumes levels of 120 decibels, more than your ears can safely handle for prolonged periods of time. Some manufacturers of these devices offer sound-limiting software, but it's up to the user to set the limits. Many hearing experts recommend they not be played higher than 85 decibels. New research and volume recommendations are still coming out; if you are interested in protecting your hearing, check current guidelines. Devices that measure decibel output are available in major electronics stores.

A WORD ON HEARING AIDS

If you need a hearing aid and hesitate because you're afraid of what people will think and you don't want to call attention to the problem, you may want to reconsider. People will appreciate efforts to hear them, and hearing aids call less attention to a hearing deficit than someone continually asking people to repeat themselves. Hearing aids have also become far less conspicuous over the years. If hearing aids aren't an option for you, be open with people with whom you deal frequently and explain the problem. That way, you won't be missing things or be non-responsive with no explanation.

If you don't have a hearing problem, you may not relate to the fact that many people do. From time to time, people you don't know will seem to ignore you when you're trying to be friendly. If they're not looking at you when you speak, it's possible they don't hear you. According to the Hearing Alliance of America, more than 24 million people in the US have significant hearing loss and about 40% are under the age of 65. Before you take a non-response personally or decide people are rude, allow for the possibility that someone simply didn't hear you.

Hearing loss may begin in childhood (and does, more commonly than ever before with the increasing high-volume usage of MP3s and iPods). Children's ears are more sensitive to sounds than ours. Fireworks displays and concerts are fun for kids, but they will still have fun if their hearing is protected with earplugs. Rebecca Z. Shafir, in *The Zen of Listening*, described the scene at a monster truck rally with children screaming and covering their ears, tears streaming down their faces, as a scene worthy of a Charles Dickens tale. The parents, of course, don't realize, but those pained faces, tears, screams, and little hands clasped hard over the ears are often the not-so-subtle signs of damage being done. For now, their ears need protection. When they grow up, they can decide for themselves whether they want to blow out their eardrums in the nightclubs.

CONGRATULATIONS!

You have graduated from the Listening 101 chapter and are ready to move beyond the nitty gritty basics to explore listening skills and challenges, beginning with some listening "rules," a series of guidelines and tips.

CHAPTER 2

STOP TALKING!

& OTHER RULES OF LISTENING

"Conversation: a vocal competition
in which the one who is catching
his breath is called the listener."

Anonymous

~ 2 ~

RULE #1: STOP TALKING

You can't multi-task speaking and listening. If you're talking, you're not listening. This rule also applies to the talking you do inside your head. If you're thinking intently about what you want to say, you're not listening to what's being said. It's an easy tendency, but it pulls attention from listening. If the conversation is complex and taking place at a rate at which you can't get your thoughts together any other way, try to slow the pace. Allow for thoughtful pauses; try pausing for a second or two before you speak. Deeper levels of communication will never be achieved by speed. It hardly seems like a coincidence that *silent* is an anagram for *listen*.

HOLD THAT THOUGHT

What do you do when a thought that you want to remember pops into your mind? You don't want to interrupt the speaker or hold it so tightly in your mind that you don't hear the speaker's words, so what can you do? If you're in a situation where jotting down a word or two to remind you is appropriate, go ahead. Before complex deliberations, it's okay to say that you may want to make notes.

If you're in a face-to-face situation and notes are inappropriate but you want to be sure to remember to make a point, try a simple memory technique. Many effective techniques use images. If you're selling copy machines and you're listening to your customer but you want to remember to tell him about your warranty, look at something nearby and picture the warranty on it. If you're standing by the copier, picture the warranty lying on top, or if your customer is wearing a tie, picture the warranty with the letters WARRANTY big on top, pinned to his tie. When he's done speaking, you'll remember you left your memory tag on his tie and when you glance at the tie you'll see it. If you want to tell him a special feature of your paper sorter as well, picture a sorter pattern on the tie or the sorter hanging from the end of his tie.

The same works in personal conversations. Make it a quick visual symbol and pin it someplace where your eyes can fall naturally. Take a snapshot and, when you have your chance to speak, go back and look at it. Any memory technique that frees your mind from repeating words in your own head will help you focus on the speaker.

RULE #2: CREATE A SPACE

Create a *physical space*. If someone has something important to tell you, it shouldn't be told in snippets between phone calls, voice mails, and every other interruption that happens by. Focus on reacting and responding to the *speaker*.

Create, too, a space *in your mind* for what the speaker has to say, a space more focused on listening than what you know or can show that you know as soon as the speaker pauses. Creating that space allows you to learn something new, while being obsessed with what you already know makes the process of taking in new information extremely difficult. Create a space *between your thoughts*. Think of listening as a form of meditation. Quiet your mind and focus your attention on listening.

The Teacup Story

A scholar with an extensive background in Buddhist studies came to study with a Zen master. The scholar immediately began to talk about his background and rambled on about the many sutras he had studied.

The master listened patiently as he began to make tea. When the tea was ready, the scholar was still talk - ing as the master began to fill his cup. The master poured until he reached the rim and continued pouring. The scholar, watching this, shouted "Stop!" as the tea poured out over the table. "The cup is full!"

The master stopped pouring and said: "You are right. Nothing more will fit into this cup. You, like this cup, are full of ideas about Buddha's Way. You come asking to learn, but your cup is full. Before you can learn, you will have to empty your cup."

A RIDDLE

What is something that everyone needs a few of but most of us have millions; all day long we give them away but our supply never diminishes; they are spring-loaded, hard to control, and have the potential to either alienate people or bring them closer—do lots of damage or lots of good—but usually do nothing at all?

Give up? You probably have them all day long about what people say, what they wear, the movie, your friend's life, what so-and-so said to so-and-so and so on—*your opinion*. Attentive listening is *not* about sitting with your finger on the opinion spring or even on the solution spring. Unsolicited opinions are fine if your relationship with someone is of a nature that you know you have an open invitation. Some relationships are like that but others aren't and cannot be forced. If your opinion has not been invited but you believe that it would be helpful, ask permission to give it. If the answer is "no," drop it.

RULE #3: HOLD YOUR JUDGEMENTS

We love to gather opinions, snap to judgments and jump to conclusions. It's like a playground where we're always king of the hill. Most opinions are bursting with emotion and you can collect as many as you'd like without putting out any effort at all. It's only natural to have opinions, but informed opinions take effort and can be more arduous to collect. As much as we'd like to believe our gut reactions and off-the-cuff opinions are the be-all-and-end-all, we don't have to be so quick to hand down judgments. How often have we passionately expressed a gut reaction only to become turned around and regret what we said after hearing more of the facts? Allow for a thoughtful pause before reacting, a space in which to ask yourself, "Do I have the whole story?" We all have opinions about other people, many of which have more to do with ourselves and our own experiences.

It's been said: "The only difference between a flower and a weed is judgment." The same is true for the differences among family members who are estranged and members who are close, the outcast and the "popular" people, or the "wacko" and the eccentric. Part of holding off judgment is suspending your "Oh, come on!" response. We can all do it; we do it for movies. At times we're so focused and open to watching events unfold that we're literally leaning forward on the edges of our seats. Now *that's* listening. Never be afraid to put your beliefs or disbeliefs on hold while someone is speaking. You won't forget them!

When someone tells you his or her version of what happened, listen. Even if it's not an objective truth, often it's important to know what the truth is to that person. Even if you feel someone's version of events is completely skewed, *that's* the version in that person's head and *that's* what he or she is reacting to.

So, when crazy Uncle Joe starts in again about his version of the way things are, let yourself be wrapped in the story. You may learn something about Uncle Joe or yourself, or, perhaps most surprisingly, about the way things are. Who decides what's crazy, anyway? When we don't listen to people because what they say is different, when we refer to the collective "they" as the authority, when we say someone's crazy for saying one thing because *everyone knows* something else, we could be missing out. Didn't *everyone* used to *know* that the sun revolved around the Earth? And wasn't it painfully obvious that the Earth was flat? Someone had to be crazy to think otherwise!

Consider broadening your acceptance of notions you might be quick to label "crazy." If a friend tells about a psychic he visited who said his mother, long gone, appeared as a ghost wearing a chiffon gown and clanky chains to say she loves him, listen. Everything doesn't have to be a debate. Okay, so in your reality ghosts don't exist. Or, maybe they do, but they don't wear chiffon and chains. Don't worry about it. Listen and allow him to share his reality. Did it make him happy? Does it hurt anyone? Can you prove it isn't true? Even if you somehow could, why would you (unless it seems he's being taken for an exorbitant chunk of change)?

What if you don't agree with someone's choices in life? If you think that the more you give your unsolicited opinion and the more unsolicited opinions you collect the more you communicate that you care, you're missing the mark. You may not like someone's choices in a career, a mate, whatever it

"Seven out of ten people I surveyed think you look fat in that outfit."

is, but occasionally, smart as you are, your opinions don't matter. This doesn't diminish the value of your thoughts and contributions; it only makes room for differing ideas and agendas to matter as well. Not *everything* is so terribly important.

According to the spiritual teachings of J. Krishnamurti, "To observe without evaluating is the highest form of intelligence."

RULE #4: DON'T BE A LABEL READER

People are unique. We tend to create labels like Liberal, Conservative, Feminist, Dead Head, Flirt, Wise Guy, and think we know what's inside. Once we label, we think we've got their number: "Oh, I see. You're one of *them*." Suddenly, we believe we know *everything* about someone, but *they* are not really *all* alike.

RULE #5: OPEN YOUR MIND

I heard a principal speak out against corporal punishment. Not long before, he had condoned it and practiced it in his school. One day, a group of children was sent to his office for fighting and, as he was hitting a boy with a wooden paddle, he was yelling with each swing, "This... will... teach... you... not... to... hit..." He had an epiphany. He dropped the paddle as he heard himself and wondered how hitting the child would teach that child not to hit.

From that moment on, he stopped demonstrating to kids that hitting is an outlet for anger and started being a role model for finding non-violent solutions. He began to learn more about the harmful effects of corporal punishment and to share what he'd learned with teachers, parents, and other principals. That one man stopping to *listen* to himself has changed lives.

Another thing that this principal modeled so publicly is the most courageous listening skill: he let go of preconceived notions long enough to allow a change of mind. It's common to take a stand

and identify ourselves by it. We are then prone to protecting that stand even when we feel an inkling that we may be wrong, a queasy feeling in the stomach, or a need to make some noise of defiance when something is put a certain way that sounds right and we wish it didn't. What is especially courageous in the principal's case is that his new stand is not only different, but critical of and apologetic for his own previous actions.

We can always defend a side to the death to save ourselves from coming up wrong. School debating teams each take a side of the issue and, no matter what individual beliefs are, each person can come up with ideas to defend the assigned side. We're all *smart* enough to be spin doctors, but the question is: Are we *wise* enough *not* to be and to, instead, maintain our authenticity even if we have to admit to being wrong?

While we may not consciously feel the need to be right, we tend to have certain ideas about reality and feel groundless when they're threatened. Groundlessness now and then isn't a bad thing. Without it we can't break new ground or find common ground; it's okay to be unsure.

The interesting thing about being able to change your mind after listening to the other side (if the argument is truly compelling to you) is that for all the strength it takes, change is often seen as weakness. That is, unless it fits in with what we see as a common, acceptable societal pattern, such as becoming more conservative with age. We generally call people who change their minds "wishy washy." We say "Aha! But you said…" and don't have lots of respect for the answer: "I changed my mind because…" This societal belief that a person who can change his or her mind is weak makes the person who is willing and able to change even stronger. Mark Twain once said: "Loyalty to a petrified opinion never yet broke a chain or freed a human soul."

RULE #6: FOCUS

When someone is speaking, focus. When every movement in the room catches your eye, your lack of focus on the speaker is clear. If someone is speaking to you about a matter of importance, practice not answering your phone or even checking to see who is calling. You'll hear the message later and the speaker will get the message that you take his or her thoughts seriously.

Certain behaviors typically show that you are listening, such as making eye contact. Realize, though, that it's possible to be overly-focused on showing that your are listening, even to the point of your own distraction. It's also possible to use these behaviors to look as though you're listening when you're not. The behaviors that follow are useful indicators and it helps to be aware of them. However, if you're paying attention, you'll likely be showing signs of focus—such as making eye contact—without thinking about it at all. Below are some of the ways we show we're listening.

Maintain eye contact.

Maintaining eye contact is important, but if you're trying to understand a complex concept and closing your eyes helps, do it. If you're in a one-to-one conversation, be sure to alert the speaker to what you're doing so he or she doesn't think you've gone to sleep! But if you are taking a nap or looking around the room, your body language is clearly saying that you're not listening.

In the US, not making eye contact has the connotation of someone untrustworthy, someone who "won't look you in the eye." But realize, too, that steady eye contact in some cultures is considered impolite or aggressive. As a general rule, make eye contact. If you sense that too much eye contact is making someone uncomfortable, ease off.

Give non-verbal clues.

Nod, lean toward the speaker, take on the general demeanor of someone who is interested.

Encourage the speaker to go on.

Especially over the phone, hearing no response feels like no one is listening. In the world of cell phones, we often don't know if we've lost a signal. A sound or a few words here and there—"yes," "I see," "go on," "uh-huh"—let the speaker know someone is out there.

Don't be a verbal trespasser.

A verbal trespasser is one who interrupts or finishes the speaker's sentences. Lovers can get away with finishing each other's sentences for a while. In fact, people even say they're *looking* for someone who *can* finish their sentences. The romance of it usually wears thin, though, and if you're not lovers to begin with, your verbal trespass probably won't be welcome at all.

Ask open questions.

Some people just aren't chatty. You may be all ready to listen, but you're only getting dribs and drabs of information. If you want to encourage the speaker to give you more information or if you want to show a hesitant speaker that you truly are interested, ask more *open* questions than *closed*.

Closed questions are basically *yes/no* questions or ones that elicit short, one- or two-word answers. "How long have you been in town?" "Did you read about the strike?"

Open questions encourage the speaker. They elicit a more detailed response than closed questions. "What have you been doing since you got into town?" "What do you think about the strike?" "What" and "Why" are usually helpful starts to open questions. Also useful are phrases that begin with "Tell me…" "Show me…" or "Please explain…"

Summarize.

Summarizing is often helpful, especially if you have had a misunderstanding, are unsure of expectations, or have just reached an agreement. Three people in a room can come away with three interpretations, as perceptions color what we hear. It's hard to unravel "You said," "No, you said," and "I was sure we agreed upon..." weeks later. Ensure that everyone is coming away with the same idea. As an artist, Quentin Tarantino enjoys the subjectivity of art. He was quoted as saying: "If a million people see one of my movies, I hope they'll see a million different movies." While art is extremely subjective, so is much of life. Our conversations are like little unscripted plays in which we take part without realizing that they are more open to interpretation than we'd like to think.

RULE #7: VISUALIZE

In some instances, all we need to come away with is the big picture. Other times, we only want to remember some key details. Visualization is a technique that can enhance listening; a picture, as they say, is worth a thousand words. (At the very least, it's worth a few!)

Some people are more visual than others. If visualization is more a chore than a help, you may not be a visual person. But anything new takes some adjustment and might take a few tries before feeling natural.

One way to use visualization is, when possible, to visualize what you are being told. If a process is being explained to you, see the process. If someone's describing an event, picture it. If you hear someone you know is in Scotland, picture that person in Scotland or in a kilt with bagpipes so when you see each other a month later, you'll ask how Scotland was and not say, "Didn't you go to... Where was it? Wait, don't tell me, I think it started with an M..." Your picture doesn't have to be realistic and you may have never seen the place, but the picture only has to be meaningful to you; it's your head.

Be creative about visualizing in your own way. Students in listening courses have come up with ideas as diverse as imagining a net with the most important pieces of information being the nodes, creating their own styles of mind maps, or imagining the story as a moving picture.

RULE #8: REMEMBER NAMES

Plan to Remember: The first step in remembering names is deciding that they are important to remember and the second is to develop the confidence not to fill your head with "I'll never remember; I'm so bad with names," as you're being told the name.

Listen Ahead: Another way to gear up for remembering a name is to listen when you're told about someone prior to introductions. When people talk to us about people we haven't met but anticipate that we will, we often let the name wash over us as though it's unimportant until we meet the person. An ounce of memory prep never hurts. If, for instance, you're hearing about someone's family or colleagues, or you're starting a new job and the people described will become your office mates; work on developing pictures of people when you hear about them or curiosities that will be answered when you meet them. You will still meet people with whom you have no association, but you'll have a few with whom you've gotten a start and you'll be placing faces with names you've already begun to know.

Repetition: Repeat the name when you are introduced. Use the name a few times in conversation; most say three times is the charm. Use it, but don't overdo it.

Unusual Names: If a name is unusual, ask for the spelling. If appropriate, exchange business cards so you can see the name in print and also have it as a reminder. Don't be afraid to ask for a name to be repeated or spelled (and your own phonetic spelling of the name in parentheses may help). People appreciate your efforts to learn and correctly pronounce their names.

Associations: Making associations is an easy way to remember names. If someone reminds you of someone else with the same name, it doesn't get easier than that. Look for a feature or character-istic that will link people to their names or maybe the name rhymes with an appropriate descriptive word. You may even associate the name with a song so the melody pops in your mind when you see the face until the name is ingrained. Associations are usually best kept in your head; Rita might not appreciate hearing your rendition of "Lovely Rita, meter maid..." every time you see her.

June Bug: I learned a name association trick in Harry Beckwith's book, *What Clients Love*, that he learned from the owner of a sports shop in Oregon. The owner, Dean, remembered everyone's first name. His trick: give each person a memorable last name.

Beckwith gives some examples: "So he never meets a *Tom, Dick, Harry,* and *June.* He meets *Tom Cruise, Dick Nixon, Dirty Harry*, and *June Bug.*" Beckwith suggests strengthening associations by noticing a common physical trait or visualizing: "Tom's teeth and Dick's nose, for example, or simply imagining that person as the made-up one—seeing Harry saying 'Make my day,' for example."

By making associations and using visuals, remembering becomes less an exercise of simply memorizing, which can be espe-cially difficult if you're learning a number of names at once.

RULE #9: QUESTION

Going into a listening situation with questions in your mind will help you remember and, often, put information into the framework of your existing knowledge.

In *The Zen of Listening*, Shafir describes a powerful exercise in mindful listening that she uses in workshops. She divides the audience into two groups to listen to a five-minute recording of radio show commentary. She asks one group to listen for the following information: the speaker's name, background, main argument, at least two supporting points, and the speaker's overall feeling about the issue. The second group is simply asked to listen. "Without fail," writes Shafir, "at least 90 percent of the group that was given specific instructions are able to recall considerably more information than the group that was told to "just listen." Hours later, at the end of the workshop, she gives a quiz that shows at least 75 percent retention in the group that listened for specific details.

Each listening situation is different and, with practice, you will learn what questions are most helpful in different situations. You might want to try this exercise yourself at home, in classes, in meetings, or as you listen to a commentary or lecture. The questions asked in the workshop—name, intention, main point, supporting points, and overall feelings of the speaker—are, in most cases, helpful for coming away with a fairly comprehensive framework.

NOTE-TAKING TIPS

Whether you're in a meeting, a class, or involved in complex deliberations, note taking can be helpful for listening, retention, and review. But have you ever been in a class where you wrote notes so faithfully that you became a machine taking dictation without absorbing much of what was said? Excessive notes can be overwhelming to review, so instead of getting the information twice (listening and reviewing) or even once (listening in the first place) you end up not getting the information at all.

That level of note taking *can* be helpful and many people find they get more out of meetings if they take the minutes. The simple act of writing wires the words to your brain in another way, feeling and seeing the words as you write. However, if the more voraciously you take notes the less you take in, practice different styles of note taking. Loosen your grip on the pen. Breathe. Tension doesn't aid in retention as much as a relaxed state of alertness.

Note taking does not require complete sentences or that you write on the lines. Often, we take complex, multi-level ideas, flatten them to lined notes, then, as we review, we read the lines trying to envision the complexity off a straight line of words. Write anywhere on the page. If drawing a symbol helps you burn a concept into your brain, draw. You might want to write a central idea in the center of the page and put supporting ideas around it to be organized later, similar to a brainstorm outline used in writing. If traditional note taking works best for you, stick with that, but put some flags in the margins or circle (or bold, if typing) key ideas as you go.

You have some shorthand that only you would understand, but if they're your notes, why not use it? Likewise, if you have a shorthand phrase in another language, use it. Your notes should be meaningful to *you*.

If you're jotting down notes while on the phone, use trigger words. A page with two columns is helpful for a complex call. In the left, you can write the heading: "Reminders" and jot down things said that you want to remember. In the right, write the heading "Questions" or "Points to Cover" and jot down notes to remind you of questions you want to ask or points you want to make. Think of your particular needs and title columns accordingly. You may prefer to have a simple "cheat sheet" of points you want to be certain to cover so that you won't be distracted by focusing on not forgetting what you want to say.

"LISTEN" TO BODY LANGUAGE

Remember that listening involves not only words, but also taking in and deciphering non-verbal messages. Crossed arms send a message of someone who is closed off or self protective. Leaning forward is an indicator of interest while leaning back often marks skepticism or disinterest.

Watch body language for clues, but be quick to clarify assumptions if you are unsure or are getting a negative message. For instance, someone might be leaning back out of tiredness or a feeling of relaxation, and crossed arms may be a habit. However, if something is wrong, people may be quicker to show it than to say it. You can see if someone has picked up the pace walking, suddenly crossed arms while you're speaking, or seems visibly frustrated. Observe. Listen. Ask. You can get a book on body language cues and learn every signal, but every signal doesn't mean the same in every situation.

I know a corporate trainer who tells of a woman in her class who sat stiffly in the back, glaring, never smiling. Nothing the trainer did during the course made this woman seem interested at all. On a break, the trainer approached the woman to ask what she thought of the course, in the hopes of engaging her interest. The woman explained that she had just had back surgery and was told she still had to attend the class and that she was in terrible pain.

The trainer was flagged by body language that there was a problem and asking allowed her to pinpoint that problem. By not only observing, but clarifying what she observed, the trainer learned that the anguished body language and facial expressions had nothing to do with her choice of material, her style, or even her bad jokes—they were in no way a response to her, but to physical pain. Body language clues are extremely valuable listening tools, but reading them can do more harm than good if we jump to "obvious" conclusions.

STOP TALKING & OTHER RULES | 41

Listeners Speak

Body Language: An Impromptu Lesson

As a new trainer, I was assigned a program for new senior-level supervisors. The first exercise was a listening test, with audio-taped instructions and a multiple choice answer sheet.

As I observed what should have been a simple test, I noticed signs of frustration, confusion, stoic determination, and a particular fondness for the erasers on their pencils. I walked around the room to see what was happening. To my utter horror, I realized I had given them the wrong answer sheet.

Once I'd caught my breath, I stopped the exercise, admitting what had happened and apologized. Instead of the discussion I had planned, we talked about listening from a non-verbal perspective: What cues told me there was a problem? How often does this go on in the organization? How could they, as supervisors, help prevent every-day problems by listening to non-verbal cues? How important is it to notice the signals of a problem before employees become frustrated, angry or confused?

In the end, they were pleased with the session and learned from the accidental lesson on listening to non-verbal cues—and I learned to be sure to integrate that valuable concept *and* to bring the right answer sheets!

Peter Tomolonis
President, Diamond Associates
Metuchen, NJ ~ www.DiamondTraining.com

RULE #10: BE AWARE

Awareness is an essential aspect of listening on many levels. We must be aware of the speaker, aware of verbal and non-verbal cues, and aware of our own listening strengths and challenges. Each of us has a unique set of challenges. As you delve more deeply, keep an open mind. You may find that the sections you're quick to say don't apply are the very sections others would ask you to read. The remaining chapters are all within the scope of Rule #10; so much of listening is rooted in awareness.

BONUS RULE: KNOW WHEN TO BREAK THE RULES

What if two people have a style of communicating that creates comfort between them and breaks all the "rules"? Who cares? If engaging in an activity makes communication easier and everyone involved is equally focused on the conversation, whatever it is you're doing is working. I once had a difficult, stilted conversation brought to flow by a slinky. We weren't making solid eye contact, and we were engaged in a secondary activity, but somehow that slinky helped us maintain a concentrated flow. I wouldn't necessarily recommend it or expect it to have the same success twice, but it was working, so we continued. If a secondary activity derails an important conversation, it's time to get back to listening basics and cut down on distractions. But if it's hard to start a conversation and something mindless that engages a connection can bring you together, go for it!

Catching Up with Conversation

Sometimes a person needs to talk but doesn't know how or where to start. In the midst of my divorce, my eight-year-old daughter needed to talk to me and I needed to hear from her, but it seemed awkward as to how and where to begin. Then it happened. One day she asked if I would teach her to play catch with a baseball and a glove.

As we began playing catch that day, I found it was easy to start the dialogue and find hours together with no one else around. As time went on, we continued playing, while exploring feelings of all kinds. Sometimes we had to take a break to cry, laugh or just enjoy the moment.

We made it through the divorce and many other stressful periods and experiences playing catch. Even now when she is home from college or I'm visiting her, we always have time for catch. Only yesterday my daughter sent me a text message thanking me for the wonderful conversation we had the day before... playing catch.

Dr. Scott Huber
Berkeley Heights, NJ

CHAPTER 3

SHORT CIRCUITS

"Congress is so strange. A man gets up to
speak and says nothing, nobody listens,
and then everybody disagrees."

Boris Marshalov

~ 3 ~

RECEPTION

Reception in listening is important on many levels, and it's critical to realize how much damage a short circuit can cause in a given interaction or a relationship. Without reception, there is no listening.

Listening is about reception, in every sense of the word.

Reception, defined:
1. The act or process of receiving
2. The quality of a broadcast
3. A social function
4. Approval or acceptance

So, what can impair the process of receiving? ...affect how clearly a message is received? ...shut down what could have otherwise been a welcoming demeanor? ...block acceptance? A number of mental *short circuits* block reception.

SHORT CIRCUITS

Short circuit, defined: the result of two points with a potential difference coming in contact; the current tends to flow through the area of low resistance, bypassing the rest of the circuit.

It happens to everyone at some time or another. We come in contact with someone to whom we can't relate at all, "two points" that have a "potential difference," and we are so set in our beliefs that when we try to make conceptual contact, we simply short circuit. We can go through an entire conversation short-circuited without even realizing it. The current of ideas flows "through the area of low resistance, bypassing the rest of the circuit."

In other words, we'll take the ideas that support what we already know, as that's the area of low resistance; the rest hits resistance (what we already believe or what some part of us wants or needs to believe).

You will find some of the many potential short circuits here and in the following chapter. Finding and fixing your own short circuits is an important step in deepening attention and improving listening skills. Once you've run the recommended "Circuit Checks," consider any other assumptions or preconceived notions that might interfere with your listening reception. Recognizing these is essential for creating a clear listening channel.

CIRCUIT CHECKS

Check your circuits regularly. Review the "short circuits" in this chapter. How often do you notice them in your communications with others?

Do you see their lips move, but dub in words from your own head?

Sometimes we hear what we expect to hear or what we want to hear instead of what is actually being said. Our brains have little translators that tell us what people "really mean" based on what we expect or what *we* might say or do. If a statement is ambiguous, do you fill in the blanks or do you ask what the speaker meant? These translators can be so smooth that we don't even realize we're doing it. The trick is to turn off our translators and *listen*.

Intonation can easily be mistaken if we don't pay attention and ask questions instead of making assumptions. If someone says the opposite of what you would expect, are you quick to assume the comment is sarcastic? Do you know the person well enough to be sure?

Listeners Speak

The High Price of Assumptions

Our minister once told us about a meeting that he had with a vendor. The vendor quoted a price, but the minister, who was hard of hearing, said, "I can't hear you." The vendor assumed that was the minister's way of implying that the price was too high. So the vendor quoted a lower price, but again the minister was not able to hear what was said. The vendor lowered the price a second time. Finally, hearing the much reduced price, the minister readily agreed, and the vendor congratulated him on his negotiation skills.

William Carter
New York, NY

Can you hear over your own ego?

Realize that everyone you meet has something to teach you. It may or may not be hard facts or what was on *your* agenda to learn, but listen wholeheartedly and you may be surprised by what you can discover.

Are you easily distracted by passing thoughts?

When it comes to speed, your mind leaves words in the dust. You can think faster than you can speak; consequently, you think faster than others speak, too. What can you do with all that extra available speed and energy?

Why not think about what you're going to say next, what you're going to do tomorrow, wonder what the speaker thinks of you, whether the speaker might want to go out for lunch, and what's up with that hairdo? You can think all those things and still probably catch the drift of what the speaker is saying. Or, you can use some of that excess brainpower to focus more intently, give energy, and take in more fully what is being said.

Losing focus at times is natural; learning to be a better listener is a process. We can always heighten our attention, but we're still only human. If you think you've missed something, it's better to ask than risk finding out that while you were smiling and nodding you were agreeing to make an important call, have guests for the summer, or take eight weeks of samba lessons. Always know what you're nodding to!

Do you make subconscious associations?

Do you color your expectations of someone's reactions based on how someone else reacted in the past? Do you think you know what someone who's cut in a similar pattern would say, so that's what you hear? Do you confuse this girlfriend with the last one, or worse, your mother? Do you confuse this marketing rep with the last one? Do you confuse this perfect stranger with your manager because they have similar mannerisms? It's a brain default that can happen when you're operating on autopilot without paying conscious attention. That autopilot response leads us to the next short circuit: holding people to their pasts.

Is your head in the past?

If you believe you know someone so well that you don't have to listen carefully, you may eventually grow distant and lose the very connection that made you overconfident in the first place. Even those we know best have inner places we haven't seen, and they may surprise us. People we know well, though, will often say exactly what we expect them to say, but let it be said. Give people the power to express themselves.

People also need room to grow or change. Someone may have had an attitude that drove you crazy and through time, therapy, or epiphany, that person changes. The best example is you. Somewhere along the line, in some way, you made a positive change. Did the people closest to you continue to treat you as though you hadn't? For a while, at least, did things you said seem to be interpreted through the veil of who you used to be?

It's hard enough to change without negative reinforcement. If you're trying to encourage positive change in others, don't defeat their efforts with statements like, "Since when do *you*…?" Let people change. We all need time to adjust to change, our own and others', and to feel confident that a shift has been made. But after a while it's time to move forward. Hear what people are saying with their words and actions *now*.

There it is again, that concept of creating space. If someone is to grow, that person needs the space to make changes without being hemmed in by your expectations of what he or she is *supposed* to be like. Yes, anything can happen in that space. People can easily make choices that you feel are contradictory to your interests (even if it's your interest on their accounts). Risk it—especially if it's coming from someone you care about.

Do people push your hot buttons?

If someone pushes our hot buttons, we tend to short circuit. It's just how we're wired. But it *is* possible to rewire.

Think about *why* something is a hot button for you. The topic might point to something you want to change, which would make the heat feel more intense. If you put your energy towards positive change, you're not buckling to pressure. *You're* making a positive change in *your* life. Forget what anyone else says. You win.

If someone's pushing your buttons over something you can't or don't want to change, or you're on your path but it will take time, focus your energies on what matters and don't be rattled. You're probably right where you need to be and well on your way to where you want to go.

If some guy at work wants to push your hot buttons, make that his problem, not yours. Let him be one of your teachers in life. You don't have to like his method, and he doesn't have to know he's teaching you, but he was assigned to the classroom of your life, for whatever reason, so make good use of him. Learn to remain calm; learn to be confident in spite of what others say; learn whether, as inappropriately as the message may have been delivered, there's a point being made; and learn to deal with the person who loves to push your hot buttons. This probably won't be the last one you'll come across.

What truly affect us are our own reactions, especially if someone is *trying* to get a rise out of us. You can save yourself from being manipulated by being in control of your own emotions.

Are you a bottom-line listener?

Bottom-line listeners become frustrated when they have to take the scenic route because they assume that there's nothing important along the way. Straight talkers are more your style, but we can't control everything and everyone around us. Guide politely, if you can, but you'll find the discussion will go a lot faster if you relax and turn off the stopwatch. In fact, a scenic talker who becomes flustered by being rushed can easily get lost, further prolonging your trip to the facts. Have you ever noticed when you're sitting in traffic and you're anxious and fidgeting, blood pressure rising, how all that stress doesn't take you there any faster?

Remember that everyone has something to teach you and all the lessons aren't always fact driven; in addition to whatever facts find their way into the story, the scenic talker is teaching you patience. You may notice, too, that as you show patience and give your focused attention, the speaker may speed up a bit and stay more on course.

The other thing you can learn from scenic talkers is that at times you need more information than you think you need. Don't dismiss "excess information" as static. Some background may be either helpful to you or important *to the speaker* for you to know. Try assuming there's a reason you're being given what you perceive to be extraneous information. It could help and, unless you're in a real time crunch, it couldn't hurt.

Do certain situations or tones of voice make you tune out?

Many of us learned to tune out as a defensive device. If a child is constantly criticized or yelled at, that child may develop methods of tuning out or finding internal places to hide. At the time, the mechanism may have been necessary for the child to make it through tough times. By the time that child grows up, defense mechanisms tend to become deeply-entrenched habits. The impetus for the shutdown may be less threatening as an adult, but the brain learned a protective measure that worked, and, whenever any situation looks or sounds similar, the shutdown is an automatic response. It is, though, a habit, and habits can be broken.

You may sense yourself shutting down when you hear or perceive the least bit of anger or criticism. Shutting down can only escalate the speaker's emotions. A strong reaction to a minor criticism or emotional expression can blow what could be a small glitch into a major fight. Listen to what's being said; understand where the criticism is coming from; try to imagine yourself from the speaker's vantage point. Realize that everything that *feels* like a criticism is not *intended* as one.

DIALOGUE SNAGS

Effective communication is the shared understanding of a message. The receiver must interpret the message as the speaker intends or the communication is not effective. Okay, that seems pretty basic. But how often is the speaker's message unclear? How often does a listening block short circuit the correct intake of information? Can you put aside what you *know* happened to unravel a misunderstanding?

Consider the following missed communication:

Max: "How long will this job take?"

Wayne: "As long as it takes."

Max: "I just asked a question!
What's wrong with you?!"

Max storms away.

The inside story: In Max's mind, his message was simply inquisitive, looking to ascertain a time frame: "How long will this job take?" Wayne interpreted the tone as accusatory and assumed Max was complaining that the job was taking too long, so Wayne answered with resentment. Max heard Wayne's response as unprovoked hostility and snapped back.

You can see what happened here, but what would Max say happened? What would Wayne say happened? Both would believe they were right. Both would feel slighted. Either one could have cleared up the misunderstanding by assuming the possibility of a misinterpretation and calmly asking the other for clarification.

Misunderstandings *will* happen. Often, it's no one's fault. If you trust someone, trust what that person tells you about his or her intentions. The changes in pitch and mannerisms that we would normally take as clues to how someone is feeling can also be completely misleading. A quickening pace and rising pitch might convey anger or impatience. The same quickening pace and rising pitch can come, also, from nervousness or excitement, so those emotions can easily be misconstrued. When unraveling a misunderstanding, look beyond your interpretation of what you heard and ask what the person's feelings and intentions were. If this is someone you trust, give weight to the answers and replay the incident from that angle. It might play like an entirely different scene.

We often think we have agreements about what words and gestures mean when there is more grey area between us than we realize. If you're talking to me and I'm nodding, am I agreeing with you or indicating that I'm following what you're saying? If I punctuate what you say with *uh-huhs*, am I agreeing or urging you to continue? We might be cut off before I can give a clear reaction, then later have a seemingly unresolvable argument about whether or not I agreed with you. It's even possible that you would insist (and believe) that you actually heard me say the words "I agree" because you so deeply internalized your interpretation of those signals. No one is lying. Yet, we have two directly opposing versions of what happened.

Here's a look at another miscommunication:

> Tom and Jeri work together and are planning to go out for a bite after work. It's nearing the end of the day and Jeri comments that she's exhausted. Tom makes the assumption that she doesn't want to go out and says, "Let's just go out another time." In Tom's mind, Jeri was dropping a hint and it was she who wanted to cancel. In Jeri's mind, Tom just canceled out of the blue. It was the workday that was tiring for Jeri and she was looking forward to going out and unwinding with Tom.
>
> *Let similar miscommunications happen a few times and see what they both have to say about who "always cancels."*

If you cannot reach the heart of an issue, realize it's possible to have a no-fault misunderstanding and let it go with no hard feelings. When people can cultivate an understanding and trust in positive intentions, they have every reason and right to assume the best of each other.

Some misunderstandings come down to subtle misinterpretations. If they occur frequently with someone in your life, it's important to put some energy into making sure you speak the same language. Make a practice, for a while, of summarizing important points or conclusions, even putting them in writing if necessary, to avert trouble down the road.

Listeners Speak

Circuit Repair

Early in my career, when I came home from a day of listening to people, the last thing I wanted was to listen to my wife, who needed to tell me about her day. After working with kids all day she wanted adult conversation. I tried pretending to listen, but quickly learned that I couldn't fool her. We learned to appreciate each other's needs. Now, when she wants to make sure I am listening, she waits for a time-out from the game I am watching, makes me look at her and repeat what I heard. It works.

George Rozelle, PhD, BCIA-EEG
Director, MindSpa Mental Fitness Center
Sarasota, FL ~ www.mind-spas.com

CHAPTER 4

MORE SHORT CIRCUITS

"**What women want:** To be loved, to be listened to, to be desired, to be respected, to be needed, to be trusted, and, sometimes, just to be held.

What men want: Tickets to the World Series."

Dave Barry

~ 4 ~

PREJUDICIAL SHORT CIRCUITS

The word *prejudice* elicits strong reactions, one of which is defensiveness. Obviously, people who feel hatred for or actively try to hurt members of a certain group are easy to identify as prejudiced. However, many well-intentioned people who would never want to hurt anyone have at least some beliefs based in prejudice. *Prejudice* comes from the Latin, *praejudicium*, meaning *previous judgment*. We all have some preconceived notions; prejudice involves judgments. Honest self assessment is a prerequisite to listening.

The *American Heritage Dictionary* defines prejudice as:

1. a. An adverse judgment or opinion formed
      beforehand or without knowledge or
      examination of the facts.
   b. A preconceived preference or idea.
2. The act or state of holding unreasonable
   preconceived judgments or convictions.
3. Irrational suspicion or hatred of a particular
   group, race, or religion.
4. Detriment or injury caused to a person by the preconceived
   unfavorable conviction of another or others.

A particular prejudice may come from being raised with certain beliefs, or it may be a perception that's taken hold as a result of a negative incident. Prejudice can seep into our psyches any number of ways. Pre-judgments interfere with reception. Think about whether you have "an adverse judgment or opinion formed beforehand or without knowledge or examination of the facts." This is not an exercise to judge yourself, but, again, honest self-awareness is key to improving listening skills. This chapter examines a few common prejudicial short circuits.

GENDER SHORT CIRCUITS

It's the old problem of Martians and Venusians trying to live peacefully together on Earth. We love the differences between us, but some of them drive us crazy. In our search for easy answers, we may lump simple individual differences in with gender stereotypes.

So many men are forever trying to "understand women," as though finding the key to one would unlock the secrets of all women. We're quick to say that women are more emotional, men are all alike, women are born listeners, and men never listen, but we all know lots of people who disprove any or all of these stereotypes.

For instance, one gender stereotype is that men try to solve problems, but women only want someone to listen. While this stereotype might be true in one case or another, we've all seen both "listener" and "problem-solver" tendencies in both men *and* women. Being sensitive to the possibility that someone may want a listener rather than a problem solver can be helpful. On the other hand, thinking that all women want a quiet sounding board all the time will keep a man from hearing a woman when she invites his advice.

Women *and* men sometimes simply need someone to listen; at those times, a good listener is more helpful than an eager problem solver. Talking to someone who is listening often brings clarity. Talking things out with someone who is not listening will not only fail to bring clarity, it will easily derail what might otherwise be a steady train of thought and leave the speaker flustered.

Listening, alone, can help empower people to solve their own problems. Asking a few questions can pull their minds out of a rut and help them to see things in a new way. Empathy is empowering. Offer helpful feedback, if it's welcomed. The speaker may be looking to you for help in finding a solution; on the other hand, this person may just want to be heard and, possibly, to sort out thoughts with you. Don't jump to a gender conclusion. Listen to the speaker's needs.

While we don't want to fall into stereotypes and we all know people who disprove them, studies support the idea that women are *perceived* to be stronger listeners. This belief is so ingrained in our thinking, that we often say men who are open communicators are "in touch with their feminine sides." One theory is that communication styles are rooted in the games we played as children. In the past, boys were typically more involved with competitive team sports than the one-to-one communication of dolls and playing house. Even now, while girls are playing sports as much as boys, not many boys are encouraged to play "girl" games.

Men and women may, in fact, tend toward different communication styles. However, focusing on those generalizations and studying them is not as helpful as focusing on individuals and becoming better listeners, overall.

"GIRLS" IN THE OFFICE

Many, many businesses, large and small, have reached equality. Men and women are working happily together as partners, coworkers, and employers/employees. But still, the majority of CEOs and government officials are men; women still make less on the dollar than men for the same job, and gender discrimination still thrives in many work places.

Listeners Speak

Are Women Better Listeners?
The Results Are In!

There is a general belief that women are better listeners than men. However, in a large sample of 467 participants (298 women and 169 men), I found no significant differences in two indicators of listening: the listening span test and the conversational listening span (CLS) test. The listening span test measures how many last words in a spoken sentence one can recall. The CLS test measured the number of ideas that one could hold active and respond to in a conversation. I like to think of it as mental juggling. Both tests indicated no significant differences between the genders.

What *was* different was the *perception* of communicative competence, which can only be measured by external indicators, as competence is perceived by the "other." We documented nonverbal responses of both men and women, measuring gestures, body movement, face gaze, smiles, laughs, head nods and head shakes. Interestingly, men and women had no differences in nodding to show understanding; however, women shook their heads from side to side significantly more, almost twice as much as men.

Who is the better listener? My study indicates that men and women have few differences. However, women do "show" that they are listening more through their head shakes.

Laura Janusik, PhD
2nd Vice President, International Listening Association
McGee Chair of Communication and Assistant Professor Rockhurst University, Kansas City, MO

Not so long ago, women in the office were called "girls," men held the important jobs, and secretaries were expected to smile and be polite about sexual harassment. We've come a long way, but I know women who say, "Not much has changed in *my* office!" What does this have to do with listening? How much attention would you give to the ideas of a *girl* in the office? How much respect do you give to the suggestions of someone whose body gets talked about more than her accomplishments or contributions? Respect is a prerequisite to listening, especially in work situations.

Today's man is forward-thinking and sees women as equals, but some men still roam the earth who resent sharing equal time with or taking direction from the "weaker sex," an attitude that can short-circuit listening on a large scale and weaken the entire company.

GENERATIONAL SHORT CIRCUITS

So many judgments, so little time! Often, younger people judge and dismiss older people based on their age; likewise, many older people judge and dismiss younger people based on their age. In fact, no matter what our age, someone is prejudging us because of it.

I know a guy in his twenties who has an ageist mental shutdown to anyone younger, even by only a year or two. He feels he's been around longer, so what would those "kids" have to tell him? Everyone's been somewhere and experienced something that we haven't. We don't learn equally and, even if we were interested in every possible category, we all have to live within the pesky restrictions of time.

I guess you can cut off paying attention to younger people about anything because they haven't been around long enough and you can shut out older people because things have changed since they were in what you consider the thick of things. Once your field is limited to your own age group, you can keep cutting from there based on background, education, race, creed, color, style, occupation, financial status, IQ, gender, and you can keep on cutting until you end up alone, but it's lonely there at "the top" of your own mountain of judgments, and you wouldn't learn nearly as much.

"KIDS" AND "OLD TIMERS" AT WORK

We now have four distinct generations sharing office space, known as: The Silent Generation, Baby Boomers, Gen X, and Gen Next. Not only are people working later in life, many are starting earlier in the more desirable jobs as opposed to "paying their dues," starting in the mailroom or its equivalent. Where we once had a ladder, now we often have people of younger generations supervising those of older generations.

Some people fall into a pattern with a few catch phrases in response to working with other generations. To say the least, these aren't helpful. When you catch yourself saying one of them, ask yourself a question that delves beneath the surface. For instance, when you say, "We tried it before; it didn't work." Ask yourself, "Could this approach have simply been before its time?" or "Was there some flaw in how it was implemented before?" or "Am I afraid of change?" When you say, "No one respects experience," ask yourself, "Do *I* respect new ideas?" When you say, "No one wants to hear new ideas," ask yourself, "Do *I* respect others' experience?" and "How am I presenting my ideas?" When you say, "Whatever!" do you honestly expect anyone *else* to care? When you say, "Doesn't *anyone* listen?" Ask yourself: "Am *I* listening?"

MANNER OF SPEAKING

We can be turned on or off by fast talkers, slow talkers, low talkers, accents, or attitudes. On one end of the spectrum are people who are judgmental of others' accents and, on the other, people who are romanced by them. Best to keep an even keel. While judging someone by an accent is an obvious short circuit, being romanced by one interferes just as much with careful listening and reasoning.

A seasoned businessman confessed to me that he had hired a man who was under-qualified and under-experienced for a job at nearly double the salary he was prepared to pay. When things turned out badly, he reassessed what made him believe this young man was worthy of such a big risk. He said he was embarrassed to admit it, but the charming European accent led him to imagine a level of sophistication that would lead the young man comfortably into the role and ultimately be good for the company. The employer ignored every sign that this man was a bad fit with his business, and he ignored signs of a confrontational personality. The accent short-circuited his listening and, by extension, his reasoning.

In another instance, a jewelry dealer with a heavy southern accent says assumptions about his slow southern drawl work to his advantage. Buyers and sellers alike assume that he's none too bright and, in negotiations, he enjoys the fact that people think they're taking advantage of him. They are less on their guard and less apt to pick up small details. The clarity of their perceptions is short circuited by their prejudgments about slow-talking southerners.

PERSONALITY CLASHES

Some people just rub you the wrong way. Perhaps they remind you of someone from your past, maybe even someone you don't remember, but there's something about them that annoys you or makes you uncomfortable. Discomfort may come from a style of body language drastically different from your own. Likely you don't even know what it is, but *whatever* it is, it irks you. Giving people a chance is a lesson in tolerance and patience and, who knows, you might even come to like them. If not, you'll at least have grown a bit and you can't always hand pick the personality types around you.

PREJUDICE BASED ON INTELLIGENCE
OR PHYSICAL APPEARANCE

If you saw a man sitting on a park bench with wildly disheveled hair, wrinkled pants, and mismatched socks, would you walk a wide circle around him to discourage him from catching your ear? Would you assume he had nothing interesting to say and choose, instead, to sit by the more intelligent looking man in the clean, pressed suit? Would you have walked right by Einstein, sure in your belief that this man would have nothing intelligent and nothing of interest to say?

Okay, what if he isn't a genius? What if he's some lonely guy who feels lost in the world and hasn't bothered to match his socks since his wife left? Does that mean he has nothing to say? Everyone has something to teach us. Remember the old adage: "A wise man listening to a fool will learn more than a foolish man listening to a wise man."

Conversely, some people are turned off by intelligence. For some, the source of the turn-off is a feeling of intimidation that comes from being self-conscious. For others, it's a sort of anti-intellectualism at the heart of which may or may not be self-consciousness. Someone once told me that his "head shuts down when some bald guy with three PhDs starts talking" and he went on to say how he can't engage in listening to anyone he finds "unattractive" or "corny looking." Imagine a world where only the hottest people have voices that can be heard. Beyond the obvious concern that this scene is kind of creepy, I hope they have what it takes to run the world without any input from the rest of us. Speaking of the rest of us, I don't know where that leaves us. Hiding in cellars or caves? Seen but not heard or heard but not seen? Maybe we'll be allowed on radio.

While this young man's perception was extreme, a bias toward people who are seen as attractive in both social and business situations has been shown in a number of studies and experiments. Why would this be? What drives so many people to give more attention to "attractive" people? According to *Scientific American Mind* magazine, studies suggest that most people tend to find what is most typical most attractive. In the article, "Venus in Repose" by Kurt Kleiner, the author explains: "If we see some someone attractive, we say he or she is 'easy on the eyes.' Now new research suggests that beautiful faces, paintings, objects or patterns are attractive because they are easy on the mind." The article refers to a study in which people found the most "attractive" photographs to be digital composites which "average" many faces. Kleiner quotes University of California psychologist Piotr Winkielman, who says: "It turns out that our brains might simply *like* stimuli that do not take too much effort to process." The most above-average looking attractive people seem to have the most average features and easy-to-perceive patterns are "internally rewarding" and allow the brain, as Winkielman says, "to give itself a pat on the back."

So, if perception affects your reception, you're not alone, but awareness of this short circuit can help you catch it and broaden your listening mind. You might be wired in a way that gives you a tendency to narrow the focus of your attention, but you *can* change your mind.

INTERNATIONAL SHORT CIRCUITS

When communicating with people whose native language is different from your own, be patient. Use inviting body language; avoid hurry-it-up gestures. If you don't understand, ask for repetition or more details; if they don't understand, try rewording. Shouting and condescending tones do not help anyone.

Avoid jargon or slang and think of how idioms (e.g. put one over on someone, hit the ceiling, wet blanket, pay through the nose) literally sound when you are unfamiliar with their use as expressions. Be aware, and use language that will be understood.

Listeners Speak

Same-Language Subtitles

I was teaching English as a Second Language at a college. One day, the director called me into his office and said, "You have to help me; this Vietnamese couple is trying to speak to me." I answered, "I don't speak Vietnamese." He continued, "Please, you have to help me."

I nodded to the couple. They spoke to him in English, but he did not understand them. I repeated what they said, also in English, but more slowly and with pronunciation corrections. He understood and then answered them in English, which they did not understand. I repeated what the director said, again, slowly, and I simplified a word or two.

This went on for 20 minutes until the issue was settled. Everyone thanked me and I think they all thought I translated for them. Maybe I did!

Natalie Gast
Principal, Customized Language Skills Training
Little Falls, NJ ~ www.Language-Specialists.com

Beyond language, various cultures use gestures and tone differently. They may even seem to be agreeing when they're only trying to be polite. Don't waste your energy resenting the fact that someone has a difficult communication style you need to grasp. You need to adjust to different styles within your own culture, too, and likely within your own family. Think of challenging intercultural communication as accelerated training for broadening your listening awareness.

If someone from another culture is cutting you off, beware of labeling that person as rude. In some cultures, it is common for everyone to speak at once and people feel it gives the exchange a certain energy. One woman told me she was shocked when someone told her she was seen as rude for talking over people. "That is how we talk," she explained. To her it's only a lively discussion if everyone involved is shouting over each other.

And if information is in any way difficult to process, beware of saying, "I don't understand" before putting effort into listening. We may not even realize we're doing it. I might honestly think I *can't understand* someone when the fact is, I'm not *listening*.

LANGUAGE BARRIERS BETWEEN
SAME-LANGUAGE SPEAKERS

Think of the multiple meanings of words. Researchers looked at the approximately 800 most commonly-used English words and found 14,000 meanings. New words crop up every day; some slang used within one age range or interest group means nothing (or something completely different) to anyone on the outside. Imagine a teenager calling her grandma "phat" otherwise known as *cool* to some generations; grandma won't know the difference between this compliment and an insult!

Some words and phrases have multiple meanings and, depending on tone and body language, still more interpretations. Then sarcasm comes in and turns meaning around completely, so if you misinterpret a speaker's sarcasm, your understanding of the message is 180 degrees off.

Ambiguous words require more in the way of context. What about the word *later*? I might assume you mean later this morning when you mean end of day or tomorrow. *Later* means everything from two minutes to 20 years to never. Another cause of language short circuits is the use of jargon with someone who is not in your field or has a different knowledge base. (For more on jargon see Chapter 6: *Nobody Listens to Me.*)

In some cases, people don't even try to say what they mean and those closest to them learn not to "take their words at face value," as if communication isn't complicated enough! Even if everyone said what they meant and meant what they said, we'd still have communication mishaps. Even the spaces in between speech can be misinterpreted. Is it a long, thoughtful pause or the listener waiting to hear something different? Within the same conversation, what is a comfortable pause to one may feel like an awkward silence to another.

Never assume people "speak the same language" just because they speak the same language, and even those who do can easily miss a signal now and then.

PREJUDICE BASED ON CULTURAL
BACKGROUNDS, RACE, RELIGION

This section will be short, not to give less attention to this critical point, but because it's *so* critical that I want to state what ought to be the obvious clearly and succinctly. Prejudice based on cultural backgrounds, race, or religion short circuits listening, opportunities and freedom. It teaches children intolerance. It can make us dangerous beyond our most terrifying nightmares.

If you find yourself falling into negative stereotyping, try some simple mind shifts. Think of someone you know who defies that particular stereotype; we all know people who do. In fact, think of as many as you can. Think of yourself, too, and what stereotypes *you* might easily be labeled with that are unfair or untrue.

If you cannot get beyond these thoughts, they will always be an impediment to your listening. They will also interfere with your ability to listen to yourself. History is filled with people being manipulated into horrific actions because of fear that began as simple, "benign" prejudices. It's not enough to say, "That's how I was raised." We learn and grow by *listening to ourselves* analytically and *listening to others* with an open mind, free of pre-judgments.

CHAPTER 5

TALKTALKTALK

"There is a good chance that if you're
talking to me when I'm snoring
it means I'm bored."

Gary Shandling

~ 5 ~

SCRIPT TALKERS

Script talkers don't stop; they don't respond to you; and they don't take unscheduled breaks to allow others a chance to speak. A script talker has a huge blind spot and everyone else with something to say is standing in it. The spotlight is on the script talker who proceeds to deliver a monologue.

People may be harmlessly prone to falling into the same basic script on certain topics and that's perfectly natural, especially when that person is finding new audiences or has found a useful or entertaining way to express an idea or tell a story. We always hear stories repeated from those with whom we spend a lot of time. That's natural and everyone has stories to tell, but script talkers are tied to their lines. Some script talkers have a particular topic that they choose and some people are just very, very chatty regardless of topic.

Some people who do this are acting out of social anxiety and may relax and slow down when a good listener makes them feel at ease. Your first line of defense need only be to make the script talker comfortable enough to move on to different subjects or risk the silence of a pause. Sticking to the script, for many, is a comfort zone, a safe space where they know what to say and how to say it or can stay within an area about which they are knowledgeable. They would rather not risk totally free-form conversation that might make them look uninformed. Try changing the subject to other things that invite simple, easy discussion. At the same time, realize that others simply want to talk about themselves or have a need to grip the conversation in a dominant way that will not be loosened by a gentle listener.

In this chapter, you will find different types of script talkers and thoughts on how to respond if creating a safe listening environment doesn't slow them down.

Look at Me! Script Talkers

This is the all-around renaissance script talker who can and will script talk on any subject. Short of background, they will embellish whatever information they have or change the subject.

I once found myself in the middle of a boring conversation that fascinated me. A woman mentioned the small village in Italy where she had lived for four years. A man, who had been there for a week, proceeded to tell us all about the village, along with a fairly detailed analysis of the people, the economy, and the day-to-day living. We never did have the opportunity to hear much from the woman on the subject, though she tried in vain a few times to interject a different point of view.

Look-at-me! script talkers need attention and will always push to be the star of the game. Give them what you can, but try to jump in and throw a few passes to someone else. When you're ready to make your exit, do so as politely as possible. Unfortunately, if you find no pause at all for a graceful exit, you might have to interrupt to say goodbye.

Woe Is Me Script Talkers

These people may take a breath and let you speak, but it won't matter what you say; the script will remain the same, day after day, pos sibly year after year. I don't think there's much you can do to advise the woe-is-me script talker, who just wants to vent—*a lot.*

By now, you've either lost interest or you're frustrated. You want to help. You keep thinking there's something you can say to save this person, but when someone is looking to be lifted up by another person, beware of taking on that role or you'll risk becoming a crutch. Then, when you pull back from being leaned on so heavily, you'll most likely be blamed for the ensuing fall. You can offer advice and alternative perspectives, but you'll only exhaust yourself if you try to fight the truth of the old adage: You can't help people who won't help themselves.

They may be stuck in crud, and for now, for whatever reason, be unable to leave the familiarity of it. Some people need to hit a lower point than you would understand in order for them to initiate a change. As much as you care, as much as you want happiness, logic, or self-esteem to prevail, you cannot write the scripts of other peoples' lives or hold yourself responsible for the paths they choose. Best advice here: respect the woe-is-me script talker's process enough not to push and don't let yourself be pulled down. You may need to, as diplomatically as possible, try changing to a lighter subject. If someone is truly stuck or depressed, suggest professional help in the kindest of ways, being clear that there is *no* shame in seeing a career listener who is trained to help people.

The-Problem-With-You Script Talkers

People whose favorite phrase is "the problem with you" are hard to listen to. My advice is to give them their day in court. Consider the possibility that somewhere in there is a valid point and you can learn something. At least once, put aside the resistance you've built to the-problem-with-you-is script talker's seemingly endless advice and opinions. Prepare yourself mentally and emotionally to listen point-by-point.

Slow the speaker down if he or she is skipping around or prattling on. Ask questions. Reflect on what you hear. Give thoughtful responses. Summarize to assure that the speaker knows you understood what was said. Thank the-problem-with-you script talker for the advice and say that you will consider what is meaningful for you. If appropriate, follow up.

If the speaker is concerned that you are in danger, you are hurting yourself or others, or substance abuse or safety are involved, then you and this person need to explore deeper means of communication and a third party, preferably a professional, is a good idea, perhaps even essential.

If the goal is to convert you to another way of thinking or to judge your choices or lifestyle, that's another matter. From here on, whether you have agreed or not, if you have given the floor and listened, there is no reason to have the same scripts fired at you. Remind the concerned party that you have already discussed the issue. The best you can do now is, "Thank you for your concern, but we just won't agree on this."

Look-Where-I-Am-Today Script Talkers

People who have achieved a great deal are proud of themselves and why shouldn't they be? Achievement is admirable. When they tell stories to inspire, they often will. Sometimes, though, the clear intent is to put others down or say, "I made it. Why can't they?" If that's the case, you don't have to stand around listening to a look-where-I-am-today-and-look-at-all-the-losers script talker. Some people need to boost themselves up on broken egos. They live in a winner/loser reality and they'll hard sell that reality because they think it raises their stock if you buy it.

Bitter Script-Talkers

Bitter script talkers want to inform everyone about how everything "sucks" and no one can be trusted. They have something bad to say about everyone they know and they want you to believe the worst about anyone you trust. I like to try to turn the conversation, if possible, or walk away. If you find yourself in an awkward social trap and you can't lighten up the conversation, defend helpless victims, or walk away, I recommend a short trip in your head. That advice may not be politically correct for a listening book, but if someone is committing verbal hate crimes and you feel you are in no position to do anything about it, it's hard to deny yourself a short head cruise, and I say, *Bon voyage!*

Political Script Talkers

Most of us have a political position and solid opinions, but these people know all they need to know, typically speak in slogans and firmly believe it is their mission to recruit *you*. Almost nothing you can say would make one of them say to someone on the other side of an issue: "Really? I wasn't aware of that." "Where did you find your information? Tell me more." To be fair to political script talkers, that's common, especially when the root of a knowledge base goes way back to a source we see as sacred and in a country so divided. It's also faster and easier to debate at the level of what we know and not continue a conversation, over time, as knowledge is acquired. It's okay to say, "I don't have enough information to have an intelligent debate on this right now. Let me look into it." Or, if you don't have time, at least acknowledging that you may not have all the information will bridge a gap between you and the speaker. Obviously, if you're looking for a smooth sailing day, comfortable work environment or festive social time, do your best to avoid religion or politics.

A WORD TO ENTHUSIASTIC SCRIPT TALKERS

As speakers, I'm sure we've all heard ourselves so caught up in a story or the excitement of a moment that we suddenly realize: *Wow! I don't think I even paused!* If it happens once in a while, no one thinks twice about it. If you're that excited and it's not a normal speech pattern to exclude people, listeners will be much more likely to get caught up in the enthusiasm than tune out.

If you're typically looking to capture and sustain attention but you treat conversations as monologues, you will likely defeat your purpose. If you look up *bore* in *The Devil's Dictionary* (Ambrose Bierce, 1911), you will find this definition: "Bore, n.: A person who talks when you wish him to listen."

Okay, you're passionate. You probably even know more than most on a given topic, but allowing others to make points and considering them can only deepen your understanding and, possibly, strengthen your knowledge base. Pausing will undoubtedly make your friendships friendlier. If you don't have a clear, logical answer to a point, maybe you have something to learn. Answers such as, "Well, that's just dumb," or "Everyone knows…" weaken your case and tell people you'd rather offend them than think things through.

Enthusiasm is fantastic, but if you charge on without a break, if you don't care what other people have to say, they won't care about what you have to say. Your enthusiasm can be infectious and inspiring. However, if you let it trample over people's inclusion in a conversation, it will turn them off to you and your message. Getting hot and bothered about it doesn't attract anyone. "The world belongs to the enthusiast who keeps cool," says author William McFee.

THOUGHT

Never be afraid to say: "You have a point," "That's interesting. I'll have to look into it," or "I'll need some time to think that over"...*and mean it!*

Part of the listening process is receptivity. We have heard enough of the other side to be firm in our views, but have we truly listened? Critical thinking is part of astute listening. True listening takes us away from autopilot responses and engages our brains.

DISAGREEMENT

Unless coming to an agreement is important, it's okay to leave disagreements unresolved, and disagreement can be as friendly a solution as agreement. Agreeing to disagree is perfectly fine and friendly. We shared our views; I still see it my way and you still see it yours. If you, as a speaker, feel offended that listeners haven't taken on your views, you will perpetually suffer what you perceive as continual personal affronts and rejections. However, disagreement is rarely a personal issue. If you get into a heated, emotionally-charged debate at a party and you have to make a choice between being right and enjoying the evening, consider throwing the fight. Happiness is the greater reward.

AGREEMENT

If coming to an agreement is important for a business or personal issue, listen to learn what's important to the other side. Creative solutions are born of listening. Making sacrifices that mean nothing to the other side only takes away from your possible gain without strengthening your position at all. Don't assume what the other party wants, *ask*. Don't just ask *what* the other party wants, ask *why*. Someone may be negotiating a point you think is nit-picky, but if you ask *why* it's important to that person, you may find out that there's more to the issue than meets the eye. Even if you cannot concede on a point, asking *why* clues you in to what is important to the other party and what concessions you could make that would be of interest.

If nervousness makes you chatter, be aware of the tendency and keep it in check. "Selling past the close" is an expression you're familiar with if you've ever been in sales. The sale is closed, everyone's happy, and you keep chattering on until you say something that causes doubt or discomfort. This concept applies to any effort toward reaching an agreement. Stay on point, think win-win, and, when you reach an agreement—*stop selling your side!*

CONVERSATIONAL COMPETITION

Conversation is not a competitive sport. Goals of one-upping, out talking, or being louder miss the point. Such competition unfairly disqualifies contributions and discounts feelings. Also, if one person is competing and the other isn't, someone will end up getting hurt, or, at the very least, left out of the game.

If you're the competitive type and like to think of conversation in terms of a sport, think of the other person as a teammate instead of an opponent. Think encouragement, inclusion, teamwork, and passing the ball.

CONVERSATIONAL POWER PLAYS

You do not gain power by making someone uncomfortable. Some people try to make others feel small in an attempt to increase their own power. So, you will find people who intentionally defy the conventions of listening. They know the listener's response can be either constructive or destructive to the speaker's comfort and focus; they choose destructive.

You're speaking and the person making the power play is looking out the window; the "listener" lets you finish and then walks away; or you make a joke and he or she doesn't crack a smile, but cuts you down with a sharp silence. This is also the person who will hear you talking, and mid-word (no mistaking that you're not through) will begin to talk over you.

Popular power plays are pretending not to hear things or openly stating a refusal to "dignify" a statement or question with an answer. Possibly from being in their own personal depression era, people who do this have a world view that is one of lack—it says there's only so much happiness, so much success, so much confidence, and so much word-space to go around. These people tend to alienate *a lot* of people. They find a way to trash everything good that comes their way, then bum out because everything good they have has been trashed. If you find yourself in a conversational showdown, take heart. When you see the game for what it is, you severely hinder anyone's ability to make you squirm.

GOD'S SALESPEOPLE

Theological ping-pong can be fascinating and fun. However, when a social situation degrades into someone trying to convert you or trashing—not only disagreeing with, but *trashing*—your deeply held beliefs, it isn't fascinating or fun.

If it's terribly important to you for others to believe what you believe, consider this: Some people earned their beliefs the hard way and those beliefs keep them balanced. Listen to what people are saying; listen to their emotion; respect their passion and faith. If you're playing religious tug of war, listen for when to let go.

Proving your spiritual beliefs is, technically, impossible and none of us will know the truth until, possibly, when we die. Imagine blowing a relationship over beliefs only to find out, in the end, we were wrong. It would be the ultimate unrectifiable oops. I think it would be equally sad if we found out we were right because, in the end, what would we win?

TALKING TO OURSELVES SIDE BY SIDE

Martin Buber—philosopher, educator, innovator, and author—defines three types of dialogue:

1. **Genuine Dialogue:** characterized by a genuine intent to commune and deepen understanding.

2. **Technical Language:** answering the need to convey objective understanding.

3. **Monologue Disguised as Dialogue:** where people stand face to face and talk to themselves.

In Buber's words: "...there is monologue disguised as dialogue, in which two or more men, meeting in a space, speak each with himself in strangely torturous and circuitous ways and yet imagine they have escaped the torment of being thrown back on their own resources."

It's easy to fall into a script-talking pattern in certain situations and chronic script talkers usually believe they are taking part in "genuine dialogue." Read your listeners. If you have to wake them up to ask whether you've gone on too long, you have probably been engaging in a monologue disguised as dialogue.

Listeners Speak

A Listener-Free Conversation

I was listening to a conversation between my dad and my friend. Well, I'm not sure if "conversation" is the right word; it implies listening and response. They were talking, each in turn, but on totally different subjects. I can't recall the exact topics, but it was as different as one talking about his marriage and the other about his long car trip—just literally taking turns talking. Each was very polite about waiting until the other was done before continuing on his own narrative. As an observer, I kept waiting for some sign that either one had an inkling of what the other was saying, but it never came. After a while, I couldn't keep from laughing and had to ask: "Does either one of you think you're having a conversation?"

Jodi Gast
Promotional Advisor, DKG Promotions
Washington, DC ~ www.DKGPromotions.com

CHAPTER 6

NOBODY LISTENS TO ME

"Praise does wonders for
our sense of hearing."
Arnold Glasgow

~ 6 ~

TURNING THE TABLES

Let's take a break from all this listening and turn the tables to consider the question of how to get people to listen to *you*. Listening is
one side of the communication coin, and speaking is the other.
Communicating clearly, speaking when others can hear you, and
having reasonable expectations are all speaking tools that aid the
listener. If you believe that people aren't listening to you or you
want to encourage better listening, it's up to you to ensure that you
are communicating effectively.

QUESTION #1

The first question to ask yourself is this: Are you confusing
listening with agreeing? If you've expressed yourself and been
understood, but the listener chooses not to take your advice, that
may not be so much a sign of not listening as a sign of free will. Put
yourself in the listener's place. You listened but didn't agree, and
now you're being told you didn't listen—your only options are
blind acceptance or being called a lousy listener! Have you ever
been in that spot? Have you ever put others there? Before you judge
others' listening abilities, be sure that your expectations are reasonable and that you're not just talking, but *listening*, too.

A QUESTION OF RECEPTION

How receptive are you to others? Consider the short circuits discussed in Chapters 3 and 4. If you are short circuiting when others need you to be listening, they will be less likely to listen to *you*. Run periodic circuit checks. Consider, also, the script talkers in Chapter 5. If that feels at all close to home, you're less than receptive to incoming messages. If your question is "Why doesn't anyone (or a specific person) listen to me?" Try shifting the question to ask, "Do *I* give people (or this specific person) *my* attention?" "Am *I* listening?"

Listeners Speak

A Singles Q & A

I was asked to give a talk to a local singles group that met at Barnes & Noble. The topic was Michael P. Nichols' book, *The Lost Art of Listening: How Learning to Listen Can Improve Relationships*. After about an hour presentation, I was bombarded with questions for an additional 90 minutes.

As I walked away from the event with a friend, I commented that there was something uncomfortable about the question session. After talking about it for a few minutes, we both realized that every question asked was not about how they could become better listeners, but about what they had to do to get people to listen to them. That may explain why they are all still single!

Ironically, one of the best ways to get people to listen to you is by providing a great role model of listening in your own behavior.

Maria F. Loffredo Roca, PhD

Past President, International Listening Association
Chair, Department of Communication & Philosophy,
Florida Gulf Coast University

TALK WHEN OTHERS CAN LISTEN

Ensure, before you speak, that the listener is in a position to listen. You might not realize that someone is otherwise engaged when you start to speak.

Before you fault the listener for not focusing, did you:

- Walk into the room talking?
- Start talking while someone was already engaged in another activity or looking for quiet time?
- Keep talking even though someone was on his or her way out or running late?

If so, the problem isn't a lack of respect *from* the listener, but a lack of respect *for* the listener. One quick way to cause a listening short circuit is to make someone feel disrespected. Also, as a practical matter, you need to have the listener's attention before you speak.

If someone is busy and you *can't* wait, say so and ask if you can have that person's attention. If you *can* wait, ask what would be a better time. Don't hang around and don't start your story. Make a time to speak—say thanks—say goodbye.

Even if what someone is doing doesn't seem important to you, it's not your call to judge unless what you have to say is urgent (or you are informing an employee or co-worker of a high-priority need). If you want people to respect what's important to you, return the favor. They will appreciate having their boundaries respected and will be more likely to listen.

AUDIENCE & PURPOSE

If you are speaking in public or pitching an idea, thinking through your audience and purpose first is especially important. Gear your points toward your purpose and your language and style toward your audience.

For instance, if you're an acupuncturist giving presentations, hoping to educate, find clients, and build associations for referrals, your presentation to traditional medical doctors will be different from your presentation to homeopaths. And if you're making a presentation to homeopaths, you'd better have an interest in and some idea of what exactly they do before you go in to ask them to be interested in you. A presentation to a potential client would, again, be different, as would a presentation to other acupuncturists. Each of those potential audiences has a different knowledge base and different goals.

Even in a simple conversation, be aware of your audience. If your listener is fading out, take note of whether you are, for example, going into grand detail about the succulent steak dinner you enjoyed to a vegetarian who's not at all likely to share your enthusiasm. If you're talking about a product you sell, stay on the level and within the area of interest of the person to whom you are speaking. You might have expansive knowledge of how, why, where, and by whom the product is manufactured, who ships it, and what year they changed from one kind of screw to another; you may know the sales records and financials; but every prospect is not interested in every nook and cranny of information. If your listener is losing interest and *not* listening, think about whether your message is aligned to your audience.

WHAT'S IN A NAME?

A salesman was once introduced to me as Phil. The person making introductions realized immediately she was unsure about whether that name sounded right and said, "I'm sorry. Is your name Phil or Peter?" He smiled and said, "Either one is fine." Wouldn't life be easy if everyone were as agreeable as Peter/Phil? But, alas, people are attached to their names and identities.

Getting peoples' names wrong is an instant turn off. If you don't remember someone's name, ask or find out from someone who knows. Not using someone's name in a conversation will go unnoticed, but don't guess! Tossing out a name and hoping it's right means you'll risk making the person feel like another face in the crowd—unimportant, unmemorable, and interchangeable.

Saying the name right is as important as saying the right name. Harry Beckwith opens *What Clients Love*, with a public speaking story in which he says he was asked to speak to employees who loved his book, but he observed that they were so disinterested most were clock-watching as he spoke. His delivery was animated, his content was of interest, but after he was through, audience members walked by him as though he were "hosting a virus." He was then clued in to the fact that he had mispronounced the company president's name. With that, he gave the impression that the president, the company, and, by extension, the employees he was addressing, were unimportant to him and he lost his audience.

If the name is difficult to pronounce, work to get it right the first time and write it down, spelled correctly (and phonetically, if that helps). People who have unusual names that are often mispronounced will generally appreciate your efforts.

RAPPORT AND YOUR AUDIENCE

Small talk is typically used to build rapport. However, if you're trying hard to build rapport with small talk and you notice your audience has moved from discernable interest to leaning back, arms crossed, rolling eyes, what do you do? Wrong response: Try harder at the same technique, being almost aggressively friendly and hammering away to build rapport. (You'll probably notice your audience leaning back more with each wave of renewed effort.) Right response: Stop. Go directly to the point. You may be trying to be likeable and accommodating. To this bottom-line listener, you seem unable to find your way to the point and, possibly, as though you've got something to hide.

A POSITIVE SPIN

"Good morning Little Piglet…If it is a good morning…Which I doubt…Not that it matters." That's a good morning from Eeyore of Winnie the Pooh. Advice from Eeyore: "If you've been invited to a party, it's probably a mistake. Make sure they don't blame you if it rains."

If you're in a constant negative state, people will tune you out for self-preservation. Say you're working on a project with a tight timeline and you come in with your negative Eeyoresque good morning and add to the tension with uninspiring statements like: "It'll never happen!" "It can't be done!" It's disheartening. If it honestly can't be done, be realistic and talk contingency plans. But if you think it can be accomplished, albeit on a tight schedule, stay focused on making it happen.

Some people even use negative words to express positive feelings. People tend to be turned off to lots of negatives. Try choosing words that are positive. Instead of saying: "I guess it *won't be impos-sible* to finish the project," try a positive spin: "It's going to be a challenge, but it *is* possible."

Beyond being tuned out because of the deflating nature of negativity, naysayers will also find people not listening because chronic negative opinions lack credibility. If you're *always* saying the thing *can't* be done, when most often it *can*, why should we believe you this time? If you're always saying the sky is falling, people stop looking up after a while.

A positive spin also helps if you have something critical to say. If possible, start by reinforcing your appreciation for something positive. People will be more receptive to criticism if they feel appreciated for what they're doing *right*.

DEATH BY DETAILS

We can all be overwhelmed when we're getting too many intricate details that we don't want to hear. Some people can't handle hearing every gruesome detail of a surgery; be sensitive to their signals that it's too much. Or maybe you've had a health breakthrough and the people closest to you are interested in the unabridged story of your bowels; be sensitive to the fact that it may not be of interest to everyone and even those who care most may not care over dinner.

If your listeners tend to fade, think of how much information you may be giving them that they'd rather tune out. Frequently, listeners fade from too much detail because the subject is of no interest to them. Be aware of signals or blatant attempts to change the subject.

If people are generally impatient or act as though they should be able to pick and choose the details you'll share about a story that interests them, you shouldn't have to work that hard to filter, but still, be aware of your audience. I'm not advocating extreme self-censorship to accommodate everyone at every moment. However, when the entire long story (or winding side trip) is of no interest at all and you see that, be kind to the listener, cut to the chase and move on.

Beware of launching into a long, detailed story about the everyday trials and tribulations of someone you know whom the listener has never met and may never meet. If you have friends who know other friends only through your stories and those third-party "acquaintances" who've never even seen each other know more intimate details of one another's lives than, perhaps, their own families, you may be giving more details than anyone would want you to and more than most would want to hear.

In short, if your listener's eyes are glazing over, it may not be a lack of interest in you. On the contrary, the listener may be very interested in you, but not in your Aunt Molly's cousin's friend's issues with commitment. No offense to your Aunt Molly's cousin's friend. I'm sure she's very nice.

CUT THE JARGON

You may be so immersed in your field or so versed in technical knowledge that you don't realize anymore what's jargon to an outsider. It takes a higher level of sophistication to tell a complex story in simple language and not make the listener feel stupid than it does to tell the story in jargon and leave the listener behind. If you're into football, don't assume everyone knows what "feint" means (or that everyone necessarily cares). Once again, think of your audience.

Being offended that your listener can't grasp what you're saying is as illogical as getting annoyed or being condescending because this particular jargon is unfamiliar to the listener. Lots of people have lingo that would leave you at a loss, so be aware you could just as easily be in those other shoes. None of us can be a specialist at everything. It's not up to your audience to get up to speed on everything you know; it's up to you to make yourself comprehensible to the listener.

Another place to be careful is the Internet, where instant messaging shorthand has become its own form of jargon. Many people use it assuming everyone knows instant messaging lingo, but remember that it's jargon and you can easily alienate others unless you know they use it, too. For those who are unfamiliar with this shorthand, a few examples: *by the way* has

"What PART of deploying WAP applications over a Bluetooth link DON'T YOU UNDERSTAND?!"

become *btw*, *on the other hand* becomes *otoh*, *see you* is *cu*, and if you ever see a message that says *bmhatk*, that's the cyber sound of *banging my head against the keyboard*. Again, it's jargon, so only use it with those who know what it means and not those who will bang their heads against their keyboards trying to figure it out! I spoke with someone who was let in on an e-mail chain with college students and was appalled to find they couldn't spell the simplest words. She was on a tirade about the level of college education, having no idea the students were simply using a form of jargon.

CHOOSE ACCURATE WORDS

Choose your words cautiously. If you say someone "never" does this or "always" does that, you raise defenses and lose credibility. If it's important to you to point out a pattern, odds are it's more accurate to say "usually," or even "sometimes." If it's not a pattern at all, your message will be better received if you refer only to the specific incident. If someone's on trial for *everything* every time he or she wrongs you in some way, it will be nearly impossible for that person not to fall into a defensive mode. Furthermore, it's hard for listeners to wade through a litany of complaints to find and address what's actually bothering you right now.

Another language issue is words that assume intent. Phrases like: "You did this to make me feel…" or "You only say that because you want me to…" put people on the defensive. You may know how someone's words or actions *made you feel*, but that person may have had entirely different *intentions*. You will only put people on the defensive by accusing them of malicious or underhanded intent. At that point, you may not have a chance to ask what the intent was or to say what would have been most helpful to begin with: "This is how [what you said or did] made me feel."

CHOOSE DESCRIPTIVE WORDS

If your aim is to point out a problem behavior, you'll only hurt feelings and turn people off to your message by using judgments to point out that behavior. If you're dealing at home with someone who won't get a job, saying, "You're lazy," won't get you anywhere. Saying, "I noticed you haven't been looking for work. Is everything okay?" is more likely to open a discussion.

Likewise, if your aim is to encourage, you'll get more mileage from descriptive terms than from general statements of behavior. Think about which comment from the boss sounds more sincere and more like your efforts are being recognized: "You're doing a nice job." Or "I liked the creative way you handled that customer complaint this morning. Keep up the good work!" Also, a general statement that an employee is "uncooperative" would be less helpful than stating the specific actions that caused a problem and what the results were or could have been. Descriptive words inspire more cooperative results than judgments do.

WHAT'S ON YOUR MIND?

Do you say what's on your mind or do you "test" the listener? You know the package has to be there tomorrow. You stress the urgency of sending it out today (but think that you shouldn't have to add the fact that it has to be there tomorrow), so it goes out today—regular mail. If you want it sent overnight, say so. Would an attentive listener pick up your stress and know to do that or ask the question? Sure, but no one's infallible and, under stress, making sure that you're understood becomes even more important. If you don't finish your thoughts, the listener will—and the ending may surprise you. Never assume the listener can read your mind. If you want someone to listen, speak up.

Listeners Speak

I'll Tell Your Mother!

When I train or give keynote speeches, I usually hear: "I'll bet you have a great marriage since you teach and give listening training." I have to admit that sometimes I'm better at teaching and training than doing it!

I was married a year ago and was getting frustrated with my husband because he didn't help around the house. He was neater when he was a bachelor, and I was feeling like a maid. I wasn't sure how to bring this up with him, so I did what any newlywed wife would do—I called his mother. I told her about my frustrations and she said she'd talk to him for me. When he got home, he asked if everything was okay, and I said yes. He asked if there was anything I wanted to talk about, and I hemmed and hawed and finally we were talking about my frustrations. After we talked it out, he hugged me and said, "Honey, next time talk to me before you call my mother."

Lisa M. Orick-Martinez, PhD
Vice President, International Listening Association
Communication Studies Professor,
Central New Mexico Community College

WOLF CRY

Some people repeat themselves all the time and *everything* is urgent. Reasons for this include compulsion, nervousness, or lack of faith in others manifested in a persistent, "If you want something done right you've got to do it yourself" attitude. Is it possible that most people who rant and rave and repeat themselves because *no one ever listens* are absolutely right? Sure. It's the classic boy who cried wolf. After a while, people stop listening. However, you can usually win back a listening ear. Show that you're listening, show faith in others' abilities, and let some little thing go because it's a little thing.

I'D LISTEN IF ONLY SO-AND-SO WOULD TALK

You might be crowding the person you're trying to help. Imagine the space that you're creating when you listen as a physical space. If you're leaning into that space, there's no room for the speaker to come forward without feeling claustrophobic.

When someone does start to talk and you disagree with that person's perception, jumping in to correct with your belief can keep you from ever seeing the speaker's point of view. Learning what someone thinks the truth is can be as enlightening as an objective truth. Even if what you're hearing has no relation to what you know as reality, listen. What you hear is real to the person who is speaking.

SO-AND-SO IS TOO DEFENSIVE

Some people tend to be defensive; listen to their concerns and tread lightly. Some, though, simply defend themselves against actual attack. If you take the offensive and mount personal attacks, don't criticize your victim for being defensive; defending from attack is a natural, protective response.

ADVICE TO ADVICE GIVERS

If it seems no one is listening, it could be that you're talking when you ought to be listening. You will make a better case once you've taken in the other person's point of view. If you're giving advice the recipient doesn't seem to be processing and you want to throw up your hands, realize that even if *your* solution would work for *you*, that is no guarantee it will work for another unique individual at this particular time. Or, you might be mistaking someone's desire to be heard for an invitation to advise. Take some advice from the Dalai Lama: "Remember that silence is sometimes the best answer."

Another point to remember is that "should" doesn't get you very far, especially if you're "should-ing" at someone about advice you don't take for yourself. Listeners are more likely to be inspired by and less defensive about what *you've done* rather than what you think *they should* do.

Listeners Speak

The Power of Subtlety

My sister is only three and a half years older than I am, but her words have always rung true for me and she's been such a good source of information and inspiration.

Many years ago we both smoked. I was never a big smoker. I smoked so little that my internist told me it was no big deal, so I never stopped that one or two cigarettes a day. My sister arrived at my house one day, looked me straight in the eye, and said: "Phyl, I've decided that it's important for me to treat my body well. I'm in charge of that, so I'm going to stop smoking. As of yesterday, I have stopped." She didn't say to me, "You need to do this." She just said this is what I've done and this is why—I cannot abuse my body anymore. And I stopped that day. It wasn't hard for me because I only smoked one or two a day, but that's the power of words!

Phyllis Dutwin
President, Dutwin Associates
North Kingstown, Rhode Island ~ www.PhyllisDutwin.com

Your story may inspire or plant a small seed that will inspire later, or the listener may not be open at all to your message. But taking your own good advice is a start and certainly won't hurt.

SHOUT TO BE HEARD?

Talking louder or shouting when you think someone isn't listening works as well as honking your horn in a traffic jam. As tempting as it may seem, as much as shouting might feel uncontrollable *or* like the only thing you *can* control in a difficult situation, if you want to be heard, don't shout. It will only raise tensions and risk causing the would-be listener to shut down and not hear what you are saying.

WHEN IT REALLY ISN'T YOU

Other people also have their own short circuits and saturation points. They also have their own moods, distractions, and things going on in their lives at any given time of which you may not be aware.

Even the best listeners become distracted and it's no reflection on the listener or the speaker. We are, after all, only human. Remember the compassionate wisdom of A.A. Milne's Winnie the Pooh: "If the person you are talking to doesn't appear to be listening, be patient. It may simply be he has a small piece of fluff in his ear."

Someone can fall out of touch, be distracted, fade away while you're talking, or excuse himself or herself for reasons that have nothing to do with you. If you ask, you may find an explanation or, you may hear the old line, "It's not you, it's me," and it *could* be true. If someone yawns, don't take that to mean, "I'm bored with you." People get tired, and yawning is a natural response to being tired.

Consider also what you might think of as a phone snub. It's entirely possible that the reason for someone's brevity on the phone has nothing at all to do with you. Most of us have busy lives. Also, some people are phone people and some aren't, and it's nothing personal. It may be hard not to take offense because we walk around seeing everyone with phones in their ears and it seems as natural as breathing to be on one, but it isn't, really, and some people get tired of it and prefer not to be tied to it for an hour at a time.

While self-exploration is important and noticing patterns is helpful, everything that happens around you doesn't center on you (which can be a huge relief if you let it). While you examine your end of listening and communicating clearly, taking responsibility for making positive changes, it's important to realize that you only know what's happening on your own side of a given interaction.

Being aware doesn't mean straining yourself beyond all reason looking for hidden meanings or agendas. Even Freud said, "Sometimes a cigar is just a cigar."

Listeners Speak

Groggy Listening

My wife woke to see me getting ready to go to the Y for a swim at 6:00 AM. "Don't go so early," she said. I replied, "I have to because if I go any later I may have to share a lane." "Huh," she muttered, "Who's Elaine?"

Walter Ladden,
Little Falls, NJ

CHAPTER 7

LISTENING TO RESOLVE CONFLICT

"Am I not destroying my enemies
when I make friends of them?"

Abraham Lincoln

~ 7 ~

WHEN CONFLICT COMES AT YOU

We all have to deal, occasionally, with people who are angry and, whether it's personal or not, the anger is directed toward us. If your job involves taking customer complaints, you deal routinely with anger being misdirected at you. Whether at work or home, whether a misunderstanding or a mistake on your part, whether directed at you or blindly aimed, if anger comes your way, your response either feeds or defuses it.

However you choose to react, you are an active participant in any encounter you have. Whether or not you instigated someone's anger, your response has a direct bearing on whether that anger escalates or dissipates. You are in charge of determining your own reactions, and you are always taking part in creating your experiences; you also have a role in life as experienced by those with whom you come in contact. It's hard to be neutral and have no effect at all. In the famed words of Eldridge Cleaver: "If you're not part of the solution, you are part of the problem." The best strategies for defusing anger begin with listening.

THE CHOICE TO NOURISH CONFLICT

If you love conflict in your life, don't listen to anyone. Especially if someone is already hot under the collar, any sign of not listening will turn up the heat. Other ways to nurture and feed hostility include:

- A hostile reaction
- Insults
- Yelling
- Judgments or assumptions
- Self interest
- Unrealistic expectations
- Blame
- Sarcasm
- Harsh words
- Insincerity
- A "How is that my problem?" attitude
- Minimizing a problem or judging the reaction

If you would prefer to minimize angry encounters and defuse hostility, try behaviors that nourish peace instead.

"Of course we care about your business, but no one likes a whiner. Get a grip!"

THE CHOICE TO NOURISH PEACE

Listening first is the most active role you can take in defusing hostility and keeping the peace.

Listen.

The angry person's mind is heavy with how he or she was inconvenienced, cheated, mistreated, or whatever the case may be. You may want to jump in with an explanation, but your explanation may or may not be valid once you have the whole story. The angry or frustrated person needs to vent and to feel that you understand. If you don't listen first, even your best intentions won't show through and you'll look like either a head bobber or brick wall; either way, you'll appear to be someone who doesn't care. Listen with respect and empathy, the way you would hope others would to listen to you.

Validate.

If someone is fuming, there's most likely a reason. Listen carefully. Telling someone to calm down and saying that it isn't such a big deal will only escalate emotions. Obviously, the issue is of concern to the speaker, so saying it doesn't matter makes the person feel denigrated. Validate instead. Even if you have a great explanation, even if the person's expectations are unreasonable, there must be something in what this person says that makes sense and helps you understand how he or she is feeling and why. *Listen* and try to understand.

Don't act defensively.

It's hard to listen from a defensive posture and defensiveness will only fuel another's hostility. You may have a valid defense and you should be able to present it calmly, but listen first. Remember, each person's perception is his or her reality. You can't address what someone sees as reality, even if your motives have been completely misunderstood, until you are clear on that person's perceptions of the situation and your part in it.

Again, remember Rule #1 and stop talking.

Do not talk simultaneously with an angry person. The angry person will get angrier and won't hear you, anyway. Stop talking. Listen.

Ask what results this person would like.

You might refuse to give an inch because you assume people want the moon, when if you'd stop to listen, you might hear that they're not asking for so much. Discuss what you can or can't do and explain why.

If the answer is "no," say so, and explain why. If you don't know an answer, find out.

Making up answers and "yessing" people to get them to go away only worsens a bad situation.

Do not take the impersonal anger personally.

When you are dealing with angry clients or customers, they are not angry with you, personally. Your calm, compassionate behavior and a warm smile go a long way to bringing a peaceful resolution. In any situation, someone who is unhappy or disappointed may be unfairly venting at you. You *cannot* control others; you *can* control your reactions. Listen to where the anger or frustration is coming from and be part of the solution.

Take responsibility.

If you are to blame, apologize. If a person or organization you represent is to blame, apologize. Even if it's only partly you, apologize for that part. Even if you didn't mean to cause harm, but you did, apologize. Saying you're sorry doesn't mean you intended to do harm; it means that you realize you (or someone you represent) did,

Listeners Speak

Letting Go of Defenses

One of my most charged situations that led to personal real-ization about listening came when the children were young and my wife had not yet begun her graduate studies. I would come home from work, day after day, and my wife would start complaining about her day, all the problems with the children, the hassles of life at home, the housework that needed doing. It all sounded like criticism and a demand for me to help more or do something more around the house. I responded with arguments and complaints. In my defensive posture, I was focused on the fact that I already had more than enough to do at work and I already did my share of the housework. Our exchanges often escalated into arguments.

One day it struck me that I wasn't really listening when my wife complained. Instead of hearing what she was saying, I was retreating into my shell. It finally occurred to me that I didn't need to be defensive, and I didn't need to say much of anything when she complained and vented. I only need-ed to listen with sincere compassion. I began to shed my defensiveness and listen without commenting. It was an amazing moment when I discovered that it wasn't me my wife was complaining about, but rather being at home with two children all day long without adult talk and interaction. Finally, I had learned to simply listen.

(adapted from *The Art of Compassionate Listening: A Time That Helped Me Learn to Listen* presented at the 2000 International Listening Association Convention, Chicago)

Michael Purdy, PhD
Communications Program
Governors State U., University Park, IL.

however inadvertently, and that you care. Apologizing is not a sign of weakness; it is a sign of a communicative person who listens, cares, and takes responsibility. It also assures that you see the problem and will do your best not to let it happen again. That assurance builds trust and good will essential for business *and* personal relationships as long as you mean what you say and follow through. Even if you have no part in the blame and can't solve the problem, listen and empathize. Imagine you were in the same position. How would you feel? How would you want to be treated? Just your empathetic ear and support can go a long way towards helping someone.

Summarize.

Listen actively by summarizing. Summarizing along the way, during a dialogue, is helpful. If you stop and say, "What I hear you saying is..." you can check to confirm that you're understanding the speaker clearly. Allow the speaker to summarize what he or she hears, as well.

Summarizing the discussion and agreements ensures that you both leave with the same understanding. Summarize critical business dealings in writing, but consider doing the same with difficult personal matters when misunderstandings, trust or follow-through have been issues.

THE RIGHT QUESTIONS

What and *How* questions are often more useful than *Why* questions when working to resolve an issue. *Why* questions explore the cause, which can be essential to understanding and moving forward. However, *Why* is often overemphasized and could be less likely to lead to future positive action. *Why* leads to discussions of the past, rather than present and future plans of action. The "right questions" will help you elicit useful answers for finding productive solutions.

For example, asking: "*Why* didn't we find as many investors as we had anticipated?" carries the discussion to market studies, individual competencies, and Monday-morning quarterbacking of a plan. All are worthwhile, in perspective, and are certainly useful for future efforts. But if the problem is here today—we don't have the money we had counted on having—the focus needs to be on *"What* do we do now to bring in more money?" *"How* do we revise our plan to accommodate the budget we now have? *"What* is our best strategy moving forward?"

Another example is an overbooked party or event. Instead of asking the rhetorical question: "Why did we invite so many people?" ask a question that is helpful to the present circumstance: "How can we best accommodate that number of people? Ask questions that elicit problem solving or creativity—then *listen*.

Don't become so obsessed with the "right question" that your conversation becomes stilted, but asking helpful conflict resolution questions is a learning process that you can slowly integrate as you notice responses to different question types.

Remember that open questions (eliciting more than one- or two-word answers) are usually preferred by listeners who want to encourage the speaker. However, closed questions (eliciting brief or yes/no answers) have their place, too, and are often helpful in gaining an overview of a situation.

Questions to avoid altogether are those that the authors of *Looking Out, Looking In* would call "counterfeit" questions. They are insincere and not at all helpful. They come in many forms but are often transparently self serving. One type of counterfeit question is one that gives the expected answer as part of the question and is asked to attain agreement rather than an honest response or opinion: "You agree, don't you?" Another insincere question would be "Are you free this weekend?" with the hidden agenda of asking a favor. And questions like, "Are you *really* going to do what you said?" or "Do you have to disagree with everything I say?" add nothing of value to any communication and aren't helpful or enlightening to anyone.

Questions should be sincere inquiries. You won't resolve conflict by putting someone on the hot seat or hearing only what you want to hear.

REPETITIVE CONFLICT

If you're fighting with someone over every small thing, your fights probably have little to do with any small thing, but much to do with larger issues. Instead of yelling about the little things, stop. Think. What are the big things that make you or others feel insecure, unappreciated or uncomfortable in some way? What is your role in perpetuating the problem? If you've become entrenched in a pattern, you may need a third party's perspective. Either way, it's up to you to answer the hard questions, express your feelings calmly and sensitively, and to examine your own role. If you live or work in a combat zone, it's in your best interest to take responsibility for bringing about peace.

Sometimes, we want to push through in a conflict situation to be heard, but when defenses are already high, the message won't get through. Walking away—*as an agreed-upon strategy*—might be the best solution to allow both parties to come back in a calmer state of mind. For the walking-away-for-a-breather strategy to work, both parties must agree to it during a conflict-free moment.

PROBLEM RESOLUTION

Don't think you can help others or resolve issues with anyone without listening first. You may create more problems than you solve. Before you can help people get what they want, you have to know what that is, what it *really* is and not just what you would assume it to be. All great problem solvers are great listeners.

A neutral third party, whether a therapist or mediator, can be helpful in difficult situations. Especially when financial and/or emotional stakes are high, find the appropriate professional who specializes in *listening* and helping people to reach agreeable resolutions. Many look at this step as a sign of personal failure—that it "had to come to *this*," but are relieved once someone listens to both sides and helps put the problem behind them. There is no shame in seeking a professional third party who will listen to both sides. This doesn't have to be a last resort and the need to do so does *not* reflect badly on the parties seeking help. On the contrary, seeking help when needed is the sign of a proactive problem solver.

Listening for solutions through conflict and opposing desires is a complex process and much time and aggravation can be saved by calling in neutral third parties who are trained to listen. Whether you solve problems on your own or with a professional, all parties involved must agree upon the method and be invested in finding a resolution and moving forward.

Listeners Speak

Listening for Creative Solutions

My employer and I have always been able to listen to each other in negotiations and find reasonable compromises. Even when I moved out of state and became his first virtual employee, we came easily to agreements that worked for both of us. The only time we had a real problem was in negotiating my maternity leave arrangements. We quickly found ourselves at a stand-still. It was a sensitive issue and we were both so focused on singular ideas of what we felt was fair, we were each stuck on what were weren't agreeing on and not hearing where the other might compromise. I suggested calling a mediator to help us find a good, creative solution. She listened to both sides and came up with a compromise that worked out perfectly.

Jodi Gast
Promotional Advisor, DKG Promotions
Washington, DC ~ www.DKGPromotions.com

CHAPTER 8

DIVINING TRUTH

"Marge, it takes two to lie.
One to lie and one to listen."

Homer J. Simpson

~ 8 ~

THE KEY TO UNDERSTANDING PEOPLE

Ever feel as though you just can't figure people out? Here's a trick: pay attention when they speak. Listen to their words and watch their body language. It may not be fancy and it may not seem like the type of advice you'd climb a mountain to hear, but it is usually the shortest distance to "figuring people out," at least, as much as people can be "figured out."

When people tell you what they want, listen. When people tell you what they need, listen. If you don't understand, ask questions. It's a good start and so simple that we tend to overlook it and over-complicate. Sure, not everyone will say what's on his or her mind or be clear about intent, expectations, or desires, but the first, simplest step to finding out what's on someone's mind is to *listen*.

TRUTH DETECTION

If you're giving a task to someone at work and you hear the response: "I'll never get this done in time," don't just say, "Yes, you will." Sure, people may underestimate their own skills, but if the person who is expected to carry out the task truly believes it can't be done, you are getting advice from the most qualified expert in that person's abilities, schedule, and personal or professional limitations. If your response is "sure you will," without trying to work out how, when, and what else may have to happen, then you share the responsibility when the job isn't done.

If you are entering into a relationship and the other person says: "I'm no good at relationships," believe it and run fast to the nearest exit. If you're in a relationship and you hear things that don't sound right, don't pass them off as, "Gee, that didn't sound like my lover/husband/wife/friend/partner, so I guess I should let it pass. He/she just wasn't himself/herself." Find out if something is wrong; we can all understand when someone is going through a difficult time. Cut people some slack and *listen*. However, if you're making excuses often, or if the excuses you make don't even make sense to *you,* you may be cutting *so much slack* you're slacking off on looking out for yourself. Think of people as oracles of their own destinies or think of them as creators of self-fulfilling prophecies. Either way, if a potential partner, business or personal, says "I have to warn you...," pay attention. You've been warned.

The amazing truth is that some people, while still trying to carry on a lie, need to confess in some way, or brag. They will let the truth slip somehow and the more you miss the more they'll reveal until they practically tell you flat out. In the most extreme case I know of, a man was living with a woman, "borrowing" huge amounts of money, and running around with other women behind her back. She had made excuses for every red flag she saw. One day, he turned to her and said, "You know, you're a sucker." She was, to say the least, startled and asked what he meant. He said "nothing," they back-and-forthed about it a few times until finally he made a joke out of it and she passed it off thinking, "Hmm... that was odd." Months later, when the lies came out, she went over that moment (and others) endlessly, saying: "Why didn't I *listen*?!"

It happens—whether we want too much to believe or the liar is honestly that artful—but careful *listening* is the best method we have for telling truth from lies.

LIE DETECTION

Researchers at the Smell & Taste Treatment Research Foundation in Chicago, IL, compiled an index of 23 signs that show people are lying. Their research included 64 peer-reviewed articles and 20 books.

Here are a few of the signs:
- Increased incidence of leaning forward
- Licking the lips
- Touching the nose
- Averting the gaze
- Stuttering
- Clearing the throat
- Decreasing blinks
- Making errors in speech
- Using excessive pause fillers (uh, er, ummm)
- Not using contractions ("did not" vs."didn't")

Be careful not to jump to conclusions if someone is leaning forward to be attentive and licking dry lips! Remember, these are clues, not hard evidence. If someone is uncomfortable about discussing a particular topic, nervousness (even if unrelated to lying) could account for fidgeting and stuttering. And some people clear their throats a lot, no matter what they're talking about. The better you know the person with whom you are dealing, the better you can assess what is or is not a departure from typical patterns.

To test the validity of the list of signs, investigators reviewed the videotapes of President Clinton's testimony in which he denied having any relationship with Monica Lewinsky. (Apologies for dredging up the tired old Clinton-Lewinsky scandal, but it's an interesting study!) According to Dr. Alan Hirsch, the institute's neurological director, the tapes showed an increase in 20 of the 23 verbal and nonverbal signs measured in the study. Compared to a tape in which Clinton made statements known to be true, answers showed a 100% increase in leaning, a 355% increase in drinking and swallowing, a 250% increase in face touching, a 219% increase in averting the gaze and a 268% reduction in blinks. There were also, compared with fundraising tapes, significant increases in expanded contractions, speech errors, and stuttering.

Hirsch also pointed out that Clinton touched his nose approximately once every four minutes when he gave answers that later proved to be false, but barely touched his nose when giving answers that were not proven false. Nose touching is an interesting phenomenon. Lying causes a rise in blood pressure, which causes a slight swelling of nasal tissue. Hirsch calls this *the Pinocchio principle*. The swelling can cause subtle discomfort and itching, which leads people to touch their noses.

You can't always get a reading on people. The better a liar is, the harder it is to detect. A skilled liar can do it without raising blood pressure, so the Pinocchio effect wouldn't give him or her away, nor would the perfect liar be fidgeting, making errors, stuttering, and, depending on the mental state of the liar, it can be nearly impossible to tell. Even a lie detector won't work on people who "believe" their own lies.

FACE IT

Some people will say anything to get what they want; some have even studied ways of sounding believable. If you're a conscientious listener, you'll be more likely to spot inauthenticity. When we have emotional investments in people, we may want to believe them; even need to believe them, almost to a ludicrous point. It's like the Marx Brothers' movie where Groucho, caught with another man's wife, says: "Who are you gonna believe, me or your lying eyes?"

It's time to cut your losses when you hear:
"I'm sorry it's taking so long to get those contracts out to you, but I

swear to you I'm trying! You *wouldn't believe* all the technical problems we're having around here. The e-mail's down, the fax is out, and I ran out of stamps."

Or this:

(Monday) "Your website's looking fabulous! I just haven't had a chance to put it online yet." (Tuesday) "It's still not online? Hmmm... I gave that to someone to do. Let me check on that." (Wednesday) "We put it up but the server's down." (Thursday) "We're still working on getting that darn server up." (Friday) "Great news! Got the server up but we lost some of your data so we're just retrieving the backup. It'll be up soon." (Later that day) "Uh ... Crackle crackle... bad signal... crackle...I'm leaving town, crackle... but I'll have the site up by... crackle..."

Sometimes, people make the most outlandish excuses and some of us want so much to believe, we actually take to the task of finding ways the bizarre tale could be true. We'll work to convince ourselves then take surveys, asking people: "Does that sound *right* to *you*?" until we hear what we hope to hear or think we need to believe. If you have to take the survey, if your gut is bursting, if the numbers don't add up no matter how you calculate, reassess. *Listen* to the pleading gurgles of your gut. The truth is, the truth isn't that complicated.

"But sugar muffin, I *couldn't* call you from my mother's house last night. Her phone doesn't have a 3."

A RED FLAG IN DISGUISE

Too much information might be a huge red flag. It can be tricky because generally the person receiving the windfall of information thinks it's a sign of openness. So, between wanting to believe and hearing a dizzying number of details, it's easy to be taken in. If someone who is not generally chatty suddenly starts going on about what everyone was wearing, how that one said this and this one said that, giving hoards of unsolicited small details, that may be a sign of trying too hard to paint a convincing picture. If it doesn't feel like someone's natural conversation, it might not be.

THE DANGERS OF CONCLUSION JUMPING

Try to avoid starting out a conversation on the offensive. You can say some pretty ugly things before you notice your perception is up-side-down. If you are in an ongoing relationship with someone, chances are you'll work things through one way or another and that won't happen until you hear the other side. It pays to save time and save everyone involved the emotional turmoil.

If the issue is with a business associate, coworker, employee, or supervisor, jumping to conclusions can lead to serious consequences or, at the very least, undue tension and bad feelings. When you go into a conversation with the intention to confront someone, remember: if this is his/her day in court, be fair. *Listen.* Take slow, deep breaths to stay calm and focused.

If you tend to be having the same misunderstandings continually, stop running your lines like you're in a play and stop deciding you've already heard what's coming. Say, "It's time to get to the bottom of this," and put all of your attention to it. Here's an old saying worth repeating: "History repeats itself because no one listened the first time."

MORE USES FOR RULE #1

Some of us ask questions to assess a situation and then keep talking out of nervousness or angst. You're more likely to get what you want if you ask for it and then stop. If you have a problem with someone, express it, then go to Rule #1 and *stop talking*.

When you stop talking, you're not only being fair to the other person by giving a chance to respond and avoiding the pitfalls of conclusion jumping. You are also making the speaker responsible to answer you. If you put a question out there and then keep talking, you may be providing an out to someone who doesn't want to answer. If you honestly want to hear the answer, leave that space open for it, and don't be the one to jump in and fill it.

If you're absolutely certain you're being pummeled with lies, maybe you don't want to keep asking questions so much as you want to do whatever you have to do to extricate this person from your life or put some distance between you if that's possible. Whether it's business or personal, can the payoff for hanging in with someone you can't trust ever be worth it (if payoff even comes)? *Listen to that voice inside*—and don't let anyone talk over it.

YOUR WORD

It's time to time to turn the truth detector inward. What about lies told to protect others? I believe that 89.5% of lies we tell, we tell to protect ourselves. (According to comedian Steven Wright, "45.6% of all statistics are made up on the spot.") Most lies have little, if anything, to do with our heroic protection of others.

If you're lying to protect someone, ask yourself, honestly, what you have to gain or lose, and if you were in the other's position would you want—or feel you deserve—the truth? *Listen* to your answer. If you ask yourself the hard questions and you're not sure of your answers, if your head defines your actions as noble but your gut is in a knot, trust the knot.

Most of the things people lie for fear of losing—such as love, respect, being well thought of, and feeling good about ourselves—flow more effortlessly toward us when we are authentic. The more we take on the attitude that we'll do anything for love or respect, the more we do things that turn people off. You can't lie, cheat, and steal your way to healthy relationships and restful nights. The very idea reminds me of another great Steven Wright line: "I'd kill for a Nobel Peace Prize."

On the other hand is the truly unselfish lie; honesty should never take the rap for someone saying: "Wow! What an ugly baby!" Sure, we can all think of times when a white lie is appropriate. However, if someone asks "How do I look?" and your feedback would be helpful, tactful honesty can be kinder than the lie. You might say, "Now that you mention it, I don't think I'd choose a striped tie on a plaid shirt."

So, if the baby looks more like a pup to you, a lie is perfectly ethical. If the guy with the plaid shirt and striped tie is in front of a camera and asking you how he looks as the cameraman counts down, lie. If the truth puts you or someone else in real danger (and we all know when we're stretching that definition), lying becomes an act of compassion. We all know what's right.

It's *your word.* Keep it.

CHAPTER 9

LISTENING IN THE AGE OF OVERLOAD

"I'm finding this age of interruption
overwhelming. I was much smarter when
I could only do one thing at a time."

Thomas L. Friedman

~ 9 ~

CONNECTION'S DISCONNECT

Between cell phones, laptops, mini-computers—the seemingly endless array of communication gadgets—we don't stop as often to focus on each other. Listening—full-frontal, focused listening—seems a quaint old notion from when people had more time. We do seem to have *less* time for each other because we're so busy with our time-saving communication devices.

So, while we enjoy great advantages by having easy access to people at great distances, we ignore the people who are right next to us. Most of us carry cell phones and can be reached any time, which seemed great at first, but now there is no such thing as down time. We're talking on the phone as we ignore or, at best, motion to those right in front of us. As much as technology connects us, it also disconnects us more and more.

Good listeners have always been appreciated—now more than ever. The simple act of making eye contact is becoming all too rare. Some may think that this disconnect is acceptable now because we're so busy with our gadgets and phone calls, but it isn't. People are increasingly disgruntled by this rudeness. The fact that it is pervasive doesn't make it acceptable, but it does increase people's appreciation of those who still take the time to acknowledge them.

PACING

Entrainment is what happens when a number of pendulum clocks are placed in the same room—they will eventually swing in unison. If a room full of people start marching around at their own paces, they will also naturally fall into step and begin marching in unison. If we're aware of that, we can keep up when we need to, but remember our own rhythms, too. If we're not careful, we can get caught up in the ever-quickening pace to the point that it can make us anxious, depressed, overwhelmed, short tempered, even sick.

Keeping pace is obviously important in business, but keeping an unreasonable pace all the time without breaks causes burnout and is hard on the health of body, mind, relationships, and even work. Paying attention to a fax, an e-mail, a beeper, a person in front of you, and a person on the phone all at the same time is impossible. Just because we have so many gadgets and ways to be reached and they all may call to us at once, does not mean that we can or should multi-task ourselves out of real communication. Even with the myriad of advances around us, we're still human, with all of the wonders and limitations that go along with that. Conscious, focused attention cannot be divided five ways and maintain its integrity as conscious, focused attention.

If an employee or colleague is in your office talking to you about something important, unless you're expecting an urgent call, let the phone ring, ignore the dings of incoming e-mail, and don't let anything turn your attention. It's a small thing for you to do and goes a long way towards making someone feel valued and appreciated. If you are, in fact, waiting for an urgent call, say so and apologize in advance that you might have to take it. Have you ever stopped to notice how appreciative people can be simply to be listened to? You might be surprised.

DEPTH ON THE HURRY-UP

In 1899, goes the story, Charles Duell, the director of the US Patent Office, wanted to close down the office because everything that *could be* invented had *already been* invented. Our need for speed and technological prowess continues to accelerate beyond the furthest reaches of Duell's dreams. Okay, that's not saying much, but it would have been far beyond the dreams of most to think of cell phones, computers, Palm Pilots, or their continual offshoots and advances in the communication age.

As we receive information faster and faster, we develop expectations of speed and, with that, our attention spans and patience tend to get shorter. At first, we thought the dial-up Internet was amazingly fast, and now most of us couldn't bear to go back to dial-up. We want information *now*.

What is the consequence of a growing mass impatience with face-to-face communication? Are we more likely to tense up when someone pauses to think? Is there an irritable, impatient, techno-info-speed junkie inside shouting: "Spit it out!"? And what happens to depth when conversation speeds up? What happens to ideas? Intimacy? Contemplation and evaluative thinking?

We subscribe to more, buy more channels, spend more time online and think we're more informed, but we may, in fact, be less informed than we would be if we slowed down to *think*.

SOUND BYTES

We're channel surfers and Web surfers; if our interest isn't captured in a second, we're likely to surf on. Messages get shorter and flashier in an effort to grab our attention. Sound bytes are repeated over and over and we can't catch every whole story. When we do, the typical story is enormously abbreviated and often presented without much in the way of context, almost no more than a sound byte itself. The thing about sound bytes is that they don't give us much to chew on.

During political debates, our conversations tend to mimic the shallow exchange of slogans, or sound byte fights, we see on televised debates. Most of us are quick to either believe unquestioningly or totally disregard points, as debates rarely admit shades of grey or encourage complex deliberations.

SIGHT OVER SOUND

Visuals are in-your-face—literally. Their light reflection enters your eye, and they're in your brain; it's a passive activity. Certainly, we can miss seeing things that are right in front of us when we're deep in thought, but not as easily as we can let the words around us go undeciphered. As television *viewers*, many of us find ourselves tired or distracted as we take in the passing images; our listening goes in and out of focus. Even when you focus on both audio and visual, the stronger impact seems to come from visuals. Never underestimate the power of a visual. A picture, as they say, is worth a thousand words.

Lesley Stahl, in her book, *Reporting Live,* discusses the overpowering force of images. She prepared a report on how former President Reagan used television images to create an image of himself that was contrary to some of his controversial policies. (Again, apologies for using a political example, but this Stahl piece offers a perfect illustration of visual over voice.) Among the images she showed were of a smiling Reagan at the opening of a nursing home and presenting medals at the special Olympics. As the images played, her voice spoke over each relating a public policy that she described as contrary to helping those in the video.

When the piece was shown to an audience of 100, without sound, the they assumed this exposé was a political promo. Not surprising. What *is* surprising is that when it was replayed with her commentary, half of the audience maintained that Stahl's report was *positively* pro-Reagan.

The average American (reports Nielsen Media Research) watches at least four hours of television per day (and the average child watches 1000 hours per year). Seattle parenting group TIP-TOK (Tuned in Parents, Turned on Kids) points out that four hours per day adds up to "two months of non-stop watching per year and nine years of a 65-year life" and compares the 1000 hours per year the average child is watching television to 900 hours spent in school.

CRITICAL LISTENING

Are we strong enough in our own minds to keep from being swayed by visuals? Are we only listening to validate our opinions? How much are we affected by someone's looks? How much are we swayed by charisma (or lack of charisma)? How quick are we to swallow a carefully conceived sound byte without asking critical questions?

Market researchers study what persuades and motivates, what colors make us hungry and what scares us. If we're not thinking critically, we're more likely to be the subjects of market manipulation. Studies have reached new levels of looking inside our heads; the latest is the use of Magnetic Resonance Imaging (MRI) machines to gauge our desires for particular products and responses to potential marketing stimuli.

The world would be lovely if we lived in one big house of objective reality and we all acted in everyone's best interest. But people need to make a profit and it's a buyer beware world. People aren't always knowingly being deceptive, either. Many act on the facts as they know them and believe them to be, not realizing their own lack of objectivity.

One film that offers a wonderful illustration of the need to be a careful listener is *Thank you for Smoking,* in which the following dialogue took place between cigarette company lobbyist, Nick Naylor, and his son, Joey. Here, Nick tries to teach his talent for using rhetoric and pulling emotional strings to confuse an issue:

Nick: "Okay, let's say that you're defending chocolate and I'm defending vanilla. Now if I were to say to you, *vanilla is the best flavor of ice cream,* you'd say..."

Joey: "No, chocolate is."

Nick: "Exactly. But you can't win that argument. So I'll ask you: So you think chocolate is the end-all and be-all of ice cream, do you?"

Joey: "It's the best ice cream. I wouldn't order any other."

Nick: "Oh, so it's all chocolate for you then, is it?"

Joey: "Yes. Chocolate is all I need."

Nick: "Well, I need more than chocolate. And for that matter, I need more than vanilla. I believe we need freedom and choice when it comes to our ice cream and *that*, Joey Naylor, that is the definition of liberty."

Joey: "But that's not what we're talking about."

Nick: "Ah, but that's what *I'm* talking about."

Joey: "But you didn't prove that vanilla's the best."

Nick: "I didn't have to. I proved that you're wrong and if you're wrong, I'm right."

Joey: "But you still didn't convince me."

Nick: "I'm not after you. I'm after *them*."
    (Nick motions to an invisible audience.)

Who's *them*? You and me if we're not paying attention! Often we are swayed by a feeling or by words that elicit emotions or we give up our own reasoning ability to defer too easily to a so-called "expert." Listening isn't enough when speakers have their own agendas. *Critical listening* protects us from being manipulated or persuaded in ways that may be against our own best interests.

STATISTICS

Statistics show you should drink red wine, never drink, eat chocolate, not eat chocolate, tofu is good for you and tofu is bad for you, and somehow Twinkies are as healthful as broccoli—*What next?* We are overloaded with studies and statistics that seem to shift and conflict every day. How do we hold steady in this raging sea of numbers and dictates? How do we know what to believe? Evaluative, or critical listening keeps us from being swayed to the point of dizziness. Statistics can be enlightening, but they can also be misleading.

If you're looking at statistics, especially if you're considering two sets of statistics with two radically different outcomes, one important consideration is whether one source or the other has something to gain. Other considerations are who was included in the study and what variables were or were not taken into account. Before you base your life's credo around a study, realize that statistics can be confusing and, if it's a topic of importance to you, you might want to ask a few questions of your own.

When faced with a study, ask *who* (who's conducting and who's participating), *how* (how is the study conducted), and *why* (the motivation for the study). Keep in mind, too, that just because people are trying to sell you something doesn't mean their studies aren't viable, reliable, and conducted in a strict, logical manner. However, evaluative listeners who ask critical questions will be better able to discern the strength and value of a study.

Here's an illustration of how numbers can lie, even when the people conducting the study are truthfully reporting their findings. Think about the widely held belief that people in the US are living *significantly* longer now than they were 100 years ago. Statistics show that the average age now is in the late 70's while the average age 100 years ago was in the 50-year age range. Have you ever been to an old cemetery? You might see the epitaphs of people who died in their 50s, but not an overwhelming number, and you'll also see 70's, 80's, and even 90's. Averages, as you know, are taken by adding numbers together and dividing by the number studied.

We may have had some increase in life span due to medical advances, but what has changed *dramatically* isn't overall life span, but a significant reduction in infant deaths (associated with improved sanitary conditions). Actual life span statistics vary, but most include infant deaths, a factor which interferes with an accurate portrayal of a typical adult life span.

To show how inclusion of infants would skew the outcome of the average adult life span, here's a hypothetical breakdown of 100 people who might have been counted in those statistics of 100 years ago:

30 people died in infancy (lived one year or less)
5 people lived to 50
18 people lived to 69
27 people lived to 70
12 people lived to 80
8 people lived to 90

If we take the number of people in the study (100) and add their total of years lived among them (4,930), we have the average life span: 49. (For the sake of simplicity, the infant age is calculated at one year.) Looking at the numbers above from a common sense perspective, you probably wouldn't consider 49 the average life span. While reducing infant deaths is a significant, miraculous and happy achievement, it has nothing to do with average life spans of adults. If researchers took infants out of the equation and called the study "average *adult* life spans" or noted that infant deaths are not counted because they would skew the averages (if people lived beyond the dangers of infancy at that time, they were more likely to live to an actual average life span), you would see a very different outcome.

Let's take the 30 infants out of the mix. Now we're looking at a total of 70 people with a total years lived of 4900 years. Divide the number of years by 70 (the number of people) and the average age becomes 70 years. Does that seem more representative of our hypothetical group? Suddenly, the average life span jumps from 49 to 70; however, nothing has changed regarding how long the adults in our hypothetical study lived.

Another example of a popular study is the one concluding red wine is good for your health. That study may be accurate and grapes have been found to offer wonderful health benefits, but does the study take into account the variable that having a glass of red wine is associated with a relaxing, social atmosphere? People who have a glass of red wine every day are probably making that time to relax every day. What would a study yield if the control group (people who weren't drinking wine) were specifically people who take care of themselves and take time for relaxation and play? What would a study yield that measured the long-term detrimental effects of drinking alcohol every day against the cardio benefits? What would a study yield with people eating grapes (instead of drinking wine)? I don't know whether it's true that red wine is beneficial for health, but thinking about the unasked questions shows that we don't have to be wrapped in the confusion of conflicting statistics that come out daily, taking every report at face value.

Critical listening skills are empowering. They allow us to see things more clearly and not be fad jumpers who feel anxious or let down when what was good for us last week is bad for us next week. The mind is open, but aware and questioning, and the eyes are wide open, without blind rejection *or* blind acceptance.

SCIENCE FACT OR SCIENCE FICTION?

Consider this statistic from Statistics 101: *The average human has about one breast and one testicle.* Crazy, but put *all humans* into the study and take averages. The numbers add up, so who can argue? Look at 100 humans—50 men and 50 women—among them will be a total of 100 breasts and 100 testicles (one breast and one testicle, one could conclude, per human). Numbers don't lie, but they can be flexed, spun, twisted and fudged. It helps to be a savvy listener.

THE SAVVY LISTENER

In this age of overload, it is more important than ever to understand ourselves and our own listening short circuits or ways that we are—as consumers, citizens, potential investors, and individuals with deeply held dreams and fears—easily swayed.

There will always be people who will take advantage of the half-listener or the non-critical listener who is easily swayed by emotion or appearances of authority. Snake oil salesmen go way back, but now they have media access and public relations firms. How do you tell the snake oil salespeople from the good, reputable people with something that truly is "revolutionary" or honestly does have "amazing results"? How do you find the truth in a political arena filled with lies? It's impossible to always know and none of us is a *perfect* listener, but the *savvy* listener is more likely to spot the differences and less likely to be taken in.

Savvy listeners also realize that those who angle a message are not always trying to deceive; very often they believe in the truth of what they say. They have their own listening barriers and belief systems built on those barriers. A person's need to overlook certain details when listening may be deep-rooted or a necessary defense from information one might find personally threatening. Upton Sinclair once said, "It's difficult to get a man to understand something if his salary depends upon his not understanding it."

James J. Floyd, University of Central Missouri professor of communication, presents critical listening as a two-fold challenge: "One must listen critically for the purpose of self protection. But, at the same time, one must be able to detect, identify, and reject undesirable and deceptive behaviors by the other without rejecting him or her as a person of worth or value."

We all have short circuits to listening; it's important to understand that of ourselves, as listeners. We also must remember that the same is true for the speaker, even the "expert," who may have learned through careful attentive study, but may have been easily-swayed or less than open-minded in the listening and learning process. The savvy listener cannot avoid all of the pitfalls of life or always know whom to trust, and certainly we cannot know everything and must rely others a great deal, but the savvy listener is also a savvy questioner and is less likely to be misled.

CHAPTER 10

INTERNAL HEAD STATIC

"If you learn to breathe effectively, you will
improve the quality of your entire life."

Gay Hendricks

~ 10 ~

STATIC

Static, defined:

1. Random noise, e.g., crackling in a receiver or television interference, produced by atmospheric disturbance of the signal.
2. Informal.
   a. Back talk
   b. Interference
   c. Angry or heated criticism

Static is the name we give to back talk or heated criticism. Why? Because we're not listening to it. It's nothing but noise to us; it sounds like static, Charlie Brown's teacher, or something like how we must sound to dogs. Obviously, when what we hear sounds like static, we're not listening.

Noise in our heads can also be called static. Not only can head noise interfere with listening, but many distracting thoughts are also repetitive—static by nature.

STATIC THOUGHTS

A lot of what distracts us from listening attentively has nothing to do with other people or our reactions to them. Internal states affect our focus, from a bad day or sleepless night to chronic issues with stress or inner balance.

Personal Problems

Prolonged distraction interferes with the ability to listen effectively, which will, ultimately, result in more problems—damage to relationships, lost thoughts and information, and appointments or opportunities slipping by. You may need to seek a sounding board or an objective opinion. Talk to someone about what's on your mind. Maybe you need to talk the problem through or seek advice to find a different approach. Einstein said: "The significant problems we face cannot be solved at the same level of thinking we were at when we created them."

If you're going through a difficult stage, unless it is a private matter, tell people and ask their indulgence: "I may need a reminder these days, so please send me an e-mail," or "I'm sorry to be absent minded right now. Would you please repeat that?" If you're going through a difficult time—a divorce, a health problem, illness in the family—most people understand and will work with you when you find it difficult to focus and listen *if* you approach them with sincerity. Lashing out or trying to cover for the fact that you have no idea what's going on will only make matters worse.

Helping others often helps, too. Instead of saying: "She may be talking about her problems, but hey, I've got my own," listening to others gives you what might be a much-needed break from your own head.

A Bad Day

On occasion, you just have a bad day. You're drained. You're rattled. Someone is talking to you and you have no idea what's being said. It's all too much. You want to be polite, but you want the day and everyone in it to drift away. You can tell someone that it's not a good time to talk and plan a better time. People understand. We've all been there.

When It's Always a Bad Day

Okay, so you're grumpy. You've had a bad day and people should know to stay away from you when you've had a bad day. Best advice: get over it. Most likely, the people getting the brunt of your bad days had nothing to do with them. The only way you can make a bad day worse is to go on moaning about it and make pleasant people choose to avoid you. If every day seems to be a bad day, you may need to do some soul searching or seek solutions to deep-rooted or chronic problems, but shutting down or biting heads off isn't the answer.

The Grass Is Greener Syndrome

You're looking around the room for someone else to talk to, wondering if you might find something better, someone more interesting... You're scanning the room and nodding absent-mindedly. You're thinking of leaving the conversation, but you're already gone. You can't focus on what someone is saying if you're channel surfing through your brain. You might later find out you missed hearing something of interest. As long as you're there, you might as well try to listen. When you're done listening, excuse yourself and move on to those greener pastures, wherever they might be.

STATIC INTERFERENCE

What causes static interference? Causes are different for everyone and affect us to different degrees. If you're feeling fuzzy or suffering from poor concentration, many factors could be at play which may surprise you, from nutrition to allergies to stress. If you fear you have an attention deficit disorder, seek a healthcare provider's advice; also consider the common head static causes and solutions discussed in Chapters 3 and 4. In this fast-paced, high-tech society, many of us feel as though we have a disorder because we feel a growing deficit in our attention.

You might think you're losing your mind, getting old, or that you have serious problems with memory or concentration. But however complex our worlds, we may find powerful solutions in the simplest acts of focusing, breathing clean air, getting more sleep, and noticing what factors contribute to the problem. A few static interferences follow:

Noise

Silence is a radical notion these days. It's so simple, cost-free, and yet it's a rare and precious commodity in our society. We become accustomed to increasing levels of noise in our daily lives: music, talk, cell phones, computer games, traffic, and the strange concert made by music blasting out of multiple cars. Many of us don't even notice when we turn on the radio or walk into the house and flick on the television as if we're addicted to noise. I once helped someone move who would not allow the television to be turned off until the movers were in the house ready to take it. Moments of silence are restful and refreshing to the body and mind.

Nutrition

Substances that can affect mood, concentration and attention include caffeine, alcohol, sugar, drugs and chemicals. Diagnosing a food allergy might change the quality of your concentration, attention span and your life. While a certain food might be healthy and energizing for one person, it will act like kryptonite for someone who is allergic to it. Food allergies can cause both physical and emotional symptoms, including: irritability, depression, mood swings, anxiety and lethargy. If you suspect food allergies, you might want to be tested.

Food choices can also affect our brains and attention spans. You might get a headache or feel foggy or have trouble concentrating from chemical additives in your food. Another food choice that can affect attention span and concentration is a high-fat meal. While a moderate amount of healthy fats is healthy for the brain, greasy fatty foods tend to make bodies and brains sluggish. If you enjoy a lunch so heavy that eyelids droop, don't blame the afternoon meeting for being a snoozer when you can't focus.

Brain Fog

Chemicals in the air might affect concentration, as well. More and more people suffer now from "sick building syndrome" and chemical sensitivities. According to Dr. Sherry A. Rogers, author of *Tired or Toxic: A Blueprint for Health*, nutritional deficiencies or chemical exposures can cause symptoms including: "spacey, dizzy, dopey, confused, depressed for no reason, can't think straight, irritable, abnormally aggressive, and more." These are all symptoms that affect our listening ability.

If you or someone in your home or office changes emotionally, mentally, or behaviorally, if listening and focus suddenly become a chore, notice whether a new element has been introduced. For instance, new carpet, fresh paint, or strong cleaning products. Trust yourself. If you say, "I know it seems crazy, but I feel fine at home and when I go into the office I feel short-tempered and find it hard to concentrate." If your listening and concentration skills are suffering and it feels physical (and not just a raging case of "I can't stand my job"), it's not crazy and it's not in your head.

Brain fog may not be the sign of a poor listener, but symptomatic of a physical problem. If you feel your focus is impaired because of something in your surroundings, try clearing the air. Pick up a book on the effects of household and office chemicals and consider speaking with a health professional who specializes in chemical sensitivities. Early detection of a symptom can save you from more serious problems and help you find your lost focus.

STATIC CLEARING

What's the cure for all that static? We have more control over our static than we often realize. Static clearing is not always easy, but could be easier than we think and can make a tremendous difference in our capacity to listen. A few static clearing methods follow:

Breaks

Are you always on the run? Attacking new projects? Chasing down people and information? Take breaks to stretch, to walk, to think. Take lunch breaks. Go outside. Relax. Meditate or pray. Keep a journal. Laugh. Sit and do nothing. Count your blessings. Make time for friends. Visualize. Manage your time so you're not always running to catch up. Nourish relationship support systems of family, friends, colleagues, or supervisors. Do yoga, tai chi, aerobics, walking, running, sports, or dance—whatever it is that makes you feel at peace.

Choose whatever feels good to you and will keep you going back for more. Your focus will be better if you exercise and stretch both your mind *and* your body.

Sleep

Sleep is restorative. Many of us have differing sleep needs and theories abound on how much sleep we need, but we all know that if we don't get what feels like adequate sleep to us, our levels of functioning and concentration decrease. If you've ever tried to focus while sleep deprived, and most of us have, you know how important sleep is to normal functioning and processing. So, if you're sleep deprived and having a number of misunderstandings, don't be quick to blame the world until you've gotten some sleep. If you have an important meeting or presentation coming up where you want to be at your best, focused and alert, preparing all night may not be the answer. When you know you'll have to focus, plan on sleep.

When you have trouble focusing, think first about how much sleep you've gotten. We may look for complicated solutions to the problem when nothing could be simpler than the fact that humans were built with a need to shut down on a daily basis for restoration. The nervous system can't handle staying piqued indefinitely. If you think you don't need sleep because you have more important things to do, honestly assess your level of functioning. Are you trying to function on a superhuman level? You may be super, but you're still human.

Silence

Simple silence, for any length of time, even a few minutes a day, can have a powerful effect on the mind. Just a few moments without music, television, internet, phones, e-mails, to-do lists, people talking… silence.

A "Minute" of Silence

My observation is that during public gatherings, when someone asks for a minute of silence, that minute is usually no longer than 10 to 15 seconds. People become uncomfortable if it lasts much longer. They start shuffling paper, clearing their throats, moving their feet on the floor.

Kay Lindahl
Founder of The Listening Center
Long Beach, CA ~ www.SacredListening.com

Breath

When you inhale, do you breathe into your chest or your stomach? Which pattern feels more like your every-day breathing?

Chest Breathing: Abdominal muscles tighten as you inhale into your chest. Chest breathing is actually part of the fight or flight response, designed to speed breathing and put your body into emergency mode where your breath is more shallow.

Belly Breathing: Abdominal muscles are relaxed and your abdomen extends with your in breath. Belly breathing may be more in tune with the body's natural breathing pattern. Babies are born belly breathing; most of us are socialized to breathe backwards as a combination of natural stress reaction and being told to suck in our guts and puff out our chests. In fact, a natural in breath would extend your belly.

Belly breathing is a wonderful technique for relaxing and focusing. To practice breathing into the abdomen, let the breath fill your chest only after it's filled your abdomen. Take a few slow, deep breaths, filling abdomen then chest on one long in breath. Practice, when you can, incorporating this breathing pattern into your life. Even if belly breaths only remain an exercise, it's a helpful one for stress reduction. Three deep, slow belly breaths can help calm the mind, clearing the static and making us more receptive listeners.

Meditation

You don't have to be a guru to benefit from meditation (or even simple relaxation) practices. The first step to taking time out is to accept that the world *will* go on without you for a while. The second is to believe that you deserve time to nourish yourself.

If you choose to meditate, remember that it's a process. Many styles and traditions are out there. If the idea is new to you or you're looking to find a new path, you might want to look for meditation groups, classes, books or guided meditation CDs. There is no wrong way. Finding the path that feels right for you might take time, but everything you try along the way will all be part of the process. If you go off track as you meditate, don't beat yourself up—stressing out defeats the purpose. Doing something—anything—is much easier than just sitting. You might want to begin with small meditative moments or finding deep awareness in ordinary moments.

In his book, *Peace Is Every Step*, Zen Master Thich Nhat Hanh teaches how to find meditative moments in every-day events, such as sitting in traffic, doing the dishes, and even the simple act of eating a tangerine, beginning with holding it, looking at it, and visualizing its origins, back to "its mother, the tangerine tree," through rain and sunshine, blossoms and falling petals, and the growth of the beautiful fruit you are eating.

The actual eating of the tangerine can be a full experience of the senses:

> *"...peel the tangerine slowly, noticing the mist and the fragrance of the tangerine... have a mindful bite, in full awareness of the texture and taste of the fruit and the juice coming out.."*

Some of the busiest people find time to meditate because, they say, they don't have time not to. They find they are more productive and that their days and communications flow more smoothly. The clarity of mind that the process brings makes them both clearer in expressing themselves and more receptive as listeners.

So, while you may appear to be doing nothing as you meditate or practice relaxation methods, among other healthy body-mind benefits, you will be clearing static, repairing reception, and becoming more in tune with yourself and, by extension, with others. If formal meditation is not your style, simple moments of awareness, stopping to focus on your breath, and moments of quieting your mind in ways that are comfortable for you will help with static clearing.

Listeners Speak

Deep Listening

After a meditation or a yoga session, I am capable of listening with not only my ears, but with my heart and soul as well. When I am still and calm inside, I am capable of listening with my entire being.

Erin Tobiasz
Yoga and Meditation Instructor
New Smyrna Beach, FL

Clean and Clear Choices

Avoid "brain fog" symptoms by choosing non-toxic products when possible. If you must use toxic products, open windows, use fans, find a good air purifier. Clean air may help you listen better and it may even help you be around to listen longer.

TUNING IN TO SOUNDS

Silence is, as we've always heard, golden; and we are certainly richer for finding it. Sound, too, can bring us peace or joy, even bring us into deeper harmony with ourselves. Discerning sounds, finding patterns, and feeling the effects of certain sounds is a beneficial listening practice, even in interpersonal communications. Does someone's voice move you in a particular way? (What does that tell you about your communication with that person?)

What are your favorite sounds? Spend some time tuning in to sounds you may never have otherwise thought about. What sounds stir emotion, sensation, or fond memories? What sounds move you? The muffled squish of a boot in snow? The little bell chimes of cereal falling into a bowl? Children laughing? Sheets rustling on a quiet morning?

According to a compelling body of research compiled by Don Campbell, author of *The Mozart Effect,* particular sounds, rhythms, and tones can aid in healing, increase mental acuity, improve memory and learning, reduce stress, and influence one's spiritual outlook. He has compiled his own research, along with that of Alfred Tomatis, EMT specialist and sound theory pioneer, as well as a number of respected psychologists and health care professionals. Are you feeling stressed out? Among the many examples of the Mozart Effect, Campbell quotes the director of a coronary care unit, Raymond Bahr: "Half an hour of music produced the same effect as ten milligrams of Valium."

Music can also jangle the nerves or disrupt concentration, even music we enjoy. It pays to note the effects of music on your state of being. Being conscious listeners gives us the power of taking more control our moods and emotions.

Become an observer of your own listening—to music, sounds, silence. What do you notice when you stop to listen?

Listeners Speak

The Listener

I cannot see you a thousand miles from here,
but I can hear you
whenever you cough in your bedroom
or when you set down
your wine glass on a granite counter.

This afternoon
I even heard scissors moving
at the tips of your hair
and the dark snips falling
onto a marble floor.

I keep the jazz
on the radio turned off.
I walk across the floor softly,
eyes closed,
the windows in the house shut tight.

I hear a motor on the road in front
a plane humming overhead,
someone hammering,
then there is nothing
but the white stone building of silence.

You must be asleep
for it to be this quiet
so I will sit and wait
for the rustle of your blanket
or a noise from your dream

Meanwhile, I will listen to the ant bearing
a dead comrade
across these floorboards—
the noble sounds
of his tread and his low keening.

Billy Collins, *Nine Horses* (Random House)

CHAPTER 11

LISTENING TO YOURSELF

"Let your heart guide you. It whispers,
so listen closely."

The Land Before Time

~ 11 ~

DO YOU HEAR YOURSELF?

I once told someone he was the rudest person I'd ever met. He was hurt and I felt awful; I didn't think I was saying anything he didn't already know. He used to walk up to people and blurt out where he wanted to go; they were supposed to politely give him directions. Imagine being approached in Central Park by a man who says: "Strawberry Fields," then looks at you until you realize you're supposed to tell him how to get there. Well, that was my friend.

When I pointed this out to him, he replied, "I didn't say, 'Excuse me'? I thought I did. I know I said it in my head!" The best intentions mean nothing if they're not conveyed outside your head! Then we went to the Museum of Natural History, where he approached a guard and said: "Excuse me. Dinosaurs." Well, what can I say? It's a process.

YOUR WORDS

Has someone ever said something to you that hit you right in your gut? Some words pack a punch, a punch that usually flips off the listening switch to anything that follows.

Do you say things like, "How stupid can you be?" "It's not rocket science!" or "What's *wrong* with you?" What about "Shut up," or "*#%%@!" Listen to yourself. If you're in a troubled relationship, struggling to get along with co-workers, or wondering why it's so hard to engender loyalty from those around you, think about how you speak to people.

You might think people should let those comments roll off, but that's a judgment and an unreasonable expectation. Some people are sensitive and words have the capacity to cut deeply. (If you're speaking to a child, your words can echo for a lifetime.) You're intelligent. You have a broad enough vocabulary. Dealing specifically with the problem, stating expectations, showing compassion, and partnering in problem solving is not only kinder, but also more effective.

If your style of joking with your friends is to trade insults, don't assume that anyone you speak to that way will appreciate being treated as a close friend. You may think you're initiating people into your circle with friendly jabs as they wonder why they're suddenly getting jabs when it seemed you were becoming such good friends. Some people are sensitive. It's not for you to judge who's "overly sensitive," but to understand. If someone tells you that you play too rough, explain your intentions, then tone it down. If you don't, the message you're sending says that you don't care.

Overly sensitive is yet another judgment that short circuits interpersonal connections. People feel what they feel, some more than others; it's no use trying to desensitize a sensitive person. And why would you? Sensitive people are usually sensitive to others as well. They might become insensitive if they feel slighted, as people deal with hurt feelings in their own ways and not every sensitive person can claim to be a stellar communicator. If you feel put off by sensitive people or inconvenienced by having to treat someone gently, realize that it's a useful practice in softening your edges and learning to deal with different personalities. If you see the world as a cold, hard place where you can never take down your guard, you might have effectively cleared your immediate surroundings of sensitive people.

Likewise, very sensitive people have a responsibility in communications to be understanding of others' styles and to be careful not to shut down people they consider abrasive or harsh. Don't assume it's personal when it could be a personality trait that has nothing to do with you. Some people are hard around the edges for a reason and, at some point, it served them. Maybe it still does. If someone hurts your feelings, the answer is not to turn off, but to share what your sensitivities are and understand that it might be difficult for another to adhere 100% to your needs. The key is not to assume that the insensitivity is intentionally directed towards you. Someone may be thoughtless, but that way of being is often a personal style and ways of being are not so easy to adjust.

MORE THAN WORDS

Do you hear your tone of voice? Are you being defensive or argumentative without realizing it? Are you actually *yelling* the words, "I'm not yelling!"? Is your tone condescending? *How* you say things is as telling as *what* you say. Stop and listen to yourself.

What is your body language saying? If you're looking around, taking every call, distracted by every passerby, you're giving a message of disinterest. Are you listening to an idea with your arms folded and a scowl on your face? You can make a study of body language, but you can also learn a lot by paying attention to your own common sense. You can feel that's not a receptive stance. You know how it would feel to stand on the other side of crossed arms and a scowl. Are you taking a stance that says you are a receptive listener?

MEANING

Your words have meaning. Assume people are listening and choose them with care. It doesn't work to say: "I didn't mean anything by it," or the oddest line of verbal defense ever uttered, "I was *just talk - ing*." People attribute meaning to the noises we call words. If you're talking, you're saying *something* and no one is going to believe that words fell at random from your mouth.

Some people are out to offend or slip in a barb and change their minds a few words too late, and then try the "Huh?" defense. Here's how it plays out: Jack says something offensive to Jill who responds with surprise by asking, "Did you just say...?" and Jack says, "Huh?" as if acting confused will make her forget what he said or make her believe that he forgot. Nice try, Jack! As brilliant as "Huh?" sounds, don't count on it. If you put words out there, you are responsible for them.

You have the right to remain silent. Anything you say can and will be interpreted by others. Say what you mean; mean what you say. This is not to say we should all become literalists or lose our senses of humor, but we are all responsible for our words.

If you want people to *listen* to you, realize that you can't set up a pattern of "I didn't really mean that" and expect people to be open, receptive listeners when you want them to. You can't have it both ways. You cannot use half-truths and have verbal temper tantrums and gain your listener's trust.

THE POWER OF WORDS

Your words have so much power that many in the health care field talk about changing language for improved health and well being. Many link frequent use of the phrases *pain in the butt* or *pain in the neck* to hemorrhoids and chronic neck pain. That may be an oversimplification, but Louise Hay's book, *Heal Your Body A-Z*, offers a number of possible cause and effect theories connecting thought patterns with related illnesses. Whether or not you believe in the mind-body connection to that degree, it can't hurt you to stop saying, "This job is killing me," and it might even lengthen your life.

So, what is the effect of saying things like, "I'll never be happy," "I'll never get ahead," "I won't pass that exam," or "I can't relax"? A part of your brain doesn't want to make a liar out of you; you might want to try replacing negative self-talk with positive affirmations. Remember, your whole body/mind is listening.

If you try positive affirmations, some experts suggest that using present tense makes the statement feel more like a reality than a wish. Saying, "I exercise three times a week" is more powerful than saying, "I'm trying to exercise three times a week. So far I exercised yesterday, but we'll see how it goes…" Thinking of yourself and seeing yourself as someone who exercises will help you know what it looks like and create it as your reality. If you quit smoking yesterday, you're a non-smoker. Smoking is not part of who you are. It used to be, but now you don't smoke. That's not to say anything can make quitting easy, but mindset makes a big difference.

Another powerful tool is visualization. Visualize the positive outcome. If you can see it, it will be easier for you to imagine and, ultimately, create.

NEGATIVE SELF TALK

Listen to how you speak to yourself. In *The Four Agreements*, Miguel Ruiz says that we set the bar for how we allow others to treat us by how we treat ourselves. "If someone abuses you more than you abuse yourself, you will probably walk away from that person. But if someone abuses you the slightest bit less than you abuse yourself, you will probably stay in the relationship and tolerate it endlessly."

If you tend to beat yourself up about things but be very supportive of others, try listening to how you speak to others and consciously shift that kindness to yourself. When you start to beat yourself up, say, "What would I say to [someone you love & respect] if he or she did the same thing?" You might be amazed by how different your words will be. Use them on yourself. Use them in your head and say them out loud to reinforce. You're as deserving of your kindness as the person to whom you would so easily be kind.

Judgments are negative self-talk, too. I'm too fat or too skinny; my nose is big or too small, too pug or too long, too triangular, too square, too round, there's no end to the too-ness we can find. We do it to ourselves and we do it to others and it's a distraction from things that matter. Okay, so a nose may be bigger than most, let's say a big, a full-blown giant of a schnoz, but does that make it *too* big? Who's deciding what is or isn't okay? Where's the character in a cookie cutter world? *Everything* is subjective.

Do you have a daily ritual that helps you start the day feeling badly about yourself? Do you start your day by getting on the scale and calling yourself fat? If the scale triggers your bad feelings, give yourself a break and take some time off the scale. If you're dieting, you'll notice bigger changes after a week or two than you will after a day anyway. If you tend to pick yourself apart, don't magnify every tiny bump and blemish. Do your pores and capillaries look monstrous in your magnifier mirror? Throw it away! No one will ever see your pores at such magnification but a flea, and fleas don't care to judge you.

Many of us who were subject to detrimental messages or abuse (physical or verbal) from parents, peers, or teachers internalize the messages we got about ourselves. We play them back as if they've been recorded in our heads, even if the original voices are distorted or have become our own. You may have had someone telling you that you were stupid or awkward and, though the external voice is gone and no one around you thinks or expresses that, you're still playing that tape and believing it, as you have taken over the abuser's role. Worse yet, remember, you're setting the bar for how others treat you, so you may be recruiting new abusers without even realizing it. Self-talk rambles on in our heads and affects us even when we're not consciously listening or thinking about it. *Listen in* on your self-talk. Is it helpful? Is it loving? Would you talk to your friends that way?

INTUITION

We all have intuition. Put energy into listening to yourself and strengthening that intuition, learning when to listen and when not to. You may have a tough decision to make and ask everyone you know what they think. Opinions and other points of view may help you gain clarity. But we are each in charge of our own choices, and if you're hoping someone will *tell* you what you should do, it's time to stop asking others and put the question squarely to yourself.

When you come to a fork in the road of your life or the edge of an emotional cliff, the maps and calculations of the rational mind

---

Listeners Speak

Did I Say That?

Often when I rephrase and repeat to my clients what they just told me. I say: "What I hear you saying is..." They are startled by how well they really know just what they need to do but can't seem to clarify it until they have said it. They can't seem to hear themselves unless they are being listened to.

Once I had a client ranting about how one of her employees did this and that. Then she said, "I should fire her." Then she said, "Oh God, did I really just say that?" She knew what she needed to do. I didn't need to tell her. I only set up the situation in which she could hear herself.

Sandy Newman
President, Life Enhancement Coaches
Monroe, NJ

aren't enough. When you stop to listen to yourself, you'll probably find you had the answer you needed all along. Even if a goal seems beyond your reach, your intuition knows where to go and, if need be, how to defy all logic to get you there. Easier said than done, I know. But after you've done all of the rational calculations involved in making a decision, when you still feel unsure or the seemingly logical choice still feels wrong somehow, close your eyes, breathe, and listen to your intuition.

You know more of the answers to your own questions than you think you do. Then again, talking things through is helpful and a good listener will help you hear your inner voice.

LISTENING OUTSIDE THE BRAIN BOX

What if you listen to your gut and it continually misdirects you? Do you regularly make the "wrong" moves or choices that don't serve you well? Have you ever turned yourself inside-out to escape a bad situation only to find yourself right back in the same spot, even if the names and faces have changed?

If you're feeling like a doormat and every time you stand up for yourself and get off the floor you find yourself back down again, under someone's feet—or if you're continually sabotaging your own financial success, or you escape one bad relationship only to find yourself in the same situation with a different face—your intuition needs a tune up. How is that done? By listening outside the brain box. This is the time for some serious, deep listening.

Have you ever made what felt like a *radical* change and found you were in the same position? For instance, you might have an aversion to working for someone who's very high-strung because your high-strung boss worked you like you were a machine. So you switch to a very laid back boss, who's lazy and leaves the slack for you. You think you've made a 180 degree shift, but you're in the same position. You were being proactive in making a change, but somewhere along the line, you weren't listening as carefully as you might have to subtle warnings. Instead, you were listening to the voice guiding you on a path you already know.

The default mode is to make choices based on emotions that come from past experiences. The problem comes in when your future is planned on the blueprint of those emotions from the past. Sure, it's important that we learn from our pasts, but it's a very delicate listening job to recognize patterns and to look deeply at our choices and motivations.

In *Down the Rabbit Hole*, the follow-up to the popular documentary, *What the Bleep Do We Know*, Dr. Joseph Dispenza offers this explanation: "When we live by those automatic circuits that are already wired known patterns of association, we're actually not making any free will choices. We're choosing based on what we know and as long as we choose based on what we know, we'll always get what we know."

The difficulty is that as you're looking for major change, you have a vivid picture of where you've *been* and what you *don't* want, so that's easy to visualize. We can most easily create what we can recall or imagine. The challenge, says Dispenza, is this: "In order to create a new future, we have to leave the feelings of the past behind, breaking associations, focusing on an abstraction, an idea, a concept, a dream that we haven't experienced."

What this means is that we usually have more control than we realize. Embracing this idea is empowering because it allows us to break patterns and create a better future. But we only have control if we believe we do and if we listen carefully to others and to ourselves.

Step back to become an observer of your own mind. Create a fresh, vivid image of where you want to be and try to visualize it every morning. Listen to how you speak to and about yourself. Listen to how you speak to others. Listen to your thoughts in between. Watch your thoughts as though you are an objective observer. Don't judge, just notice. You may hear things that surprise you.

GOING OUT OF YOUR MIND

We all listen to the echoes of our pasts. Listening to what we think we already know is easy. However, listening outside of the loops we've already grooved into our brains requires very deep inner listening and awareness.

Can you do this all on your own? There is *no shame* in asking a third party for help. In difficult situations, most of us are too close to our own thinking to step outside and see things from another point of view or see where some mind tangle might be impeding the journey to a new way of being. If you feel stuck in the process of resolving inner conflict, a neutral listener may be of great help in finding a resolution.

In fact, working with a good therapist can deepen your listening and attention skills, guiding you to ask essential inner questions and learning to listen and respond to questions that might have been completely outside of your consciousness. The more you listen in sessions, the more a great therapist will be your partner in solving the mysteries of your mind and creating the outcomes you seek.

We all need a little help from time to time, professional or otherwise. Maybe there is someone in your life who has the wisdom and intelligence to see a critical missing piece in a puzzle you're trying to solve. But if that person is too close to the situation, as well, or if some bit of history comes between you and the wisdom offered, that is where the beauty of a *neutral* listener lies. If you're running around on the hamster wheel of your brain, slow down. Go outside of your mind to a listener who can add new levels of perspective. By doing so, you will learn to better listen to and trust *yourself*.

Listeners Speak

Listening Is Everything!

Since getting into biofeedback work I have acquired many tools to help me listen to peoples' brains and bodies. With sensors and amplifiers I can listen to the whispers from the brain and hear what is happening with that person. As part of my self-regulation approach to therapy, I teach clients to listen to their bodies. The body speaks to us first in whispers. If we ignore the whispers it speaks louder and louder until our symptoms are screaming at us. We must also listen to our inner dialogue, for the content of our self-talk determines our successes or failures as we go through life. So, it seems, listening is everything!

George Rozelle, PhD, BCIA-EEG

Director, MindSpa Mental Fitness Center
Sarasota, FL ~ www.mind-spas.com

CHAPTER 12

THE TOUCHY-FEELY SECTION

"Too often we underestimate the power of a touch,
a smile, a kind word, a listening ear, an honest
compliment, or the smallest act of caring, all of
which have the potential to turn a life around."

Leo Buscaglia

~ 12 ~

ISOLATION

In the early 1800s, the Quakers led a prison reform movement that put the prisoners into forced isolation. The idea was to encourage contemplation, thus, repentance and rehabilitation. What resulted instead was insanity. Charles Dickens wrote his observations upon visiting Eastern Penitentiary in Philadelphia:

"The system here is rigid, strict, and hopeless solitary confinement. I believe it, in its effects, to be cruel and wrong. I am persuaded that those who devised this system of Prison Discipline, and those benevolent gentlemen who carry it into execution, do not know what it is that they are doing... I hold this slow and daily tampering with the mysteries of the brain, to be immeasurably worse than any torture of the body." Humans—mentally and physically—need connection.

CONNECTION

Listening, connecting deeply with another person, does not require words. We don't always have to speak to convey our feelings. Sometimes, the person who most needs to be listened to is unable to speak. Physically or emotionally, someone may be unable to express words and that can be terribly upsetting. People in the healthcare industry are routinely faced with people who cannot speak to express themselves. The listeners among them do the greatest small deeds every day by listening to nonverbal clues, puzzling out fragmented speech, devising alternate communication methods, taking the time to listen when speaking is slow, or simply paying attention. Most of us encounter, at some point, someone whose speech is limited, whether on a permanent or temporary basis.

One day I was walking down the street when I noticed a woman sitting in her open car crying. I approached slowly, to see if she needed help. She was unable to speak, unable to stop sobbing. Then she took my hands and looked into my eyes. She didn't want to tell me what was wrong and she didn't want me to drive her anywhere. Nothing was said more than my offering to help and, after a quiet while, her expressions of appreciation. The smallest connection steadied her; she even smiled, and soon she was able to drive home. It's a terrible feeling to be alone, surrounded by people.

ATTENTION

The checkout person in the supermarket, the gas station attendant, the bank teller, the counter clerk at the drug store, they are all human beings. And, no, you don't have time to make everyone you run into during the day part of your social circle and you wouldn't want to; we only have so much time. However, it doesn't take a tremendous amount of time to look someone in the eyes and smile when you come in contact. Politely saying you're in a hurry when someone is looking to strike up a long conversation is fine, but it's dehumanizing to not be acknowledged at all. Many checkout clerks complain about people coming through on their cell phones and only listening for the total, then leaving without even a "thank you" or a smile.

Taking face-to-face connection for granted is easy as we rush through interactions to get home to our Internet connections. However, though the Internet may connect you to all sorts of people, think of the difference between seeing *lol* (the Internet shorthand for laughing out loud) and sharing the energy of laughter.

FULL SPECTRUM LISTENING

Stop talking, of course, is only *Rule #1*; listening is a full-spectrum event. Laura Janusik, a Rockhurst University assistant professor of communication, points out that the ability to empathize, see from the other's point of view, and remember and act upon what was said is essential, especially in personal relationships. The importance of full-spectrum, empathetic listening is especially evident in relationships in which we feel most connected to others, such as close friends or romantic partners. We need to feel that others are doing more than listening and responding, but honestly connecting and taking the message in. We all want to be listened to and understood. Even if we don't fully understand, making the effort, asking questions, and learning to empathize (even when someone's choices are different from what our own would be) is at the heart of all healthy, supportive relationships.

THE BENEFIT OF THE DOUBT

Everyone has a story. We often decide someone is interesting or worthy of our respect after we hear a story about that person that reaches out and grabs our attention. You don't have to first hear their stories to know that people have been through tough stages, been heroic at times, or given of themselves for others. Assume they have. At some time, most people have.

Another common assumption is that quiet ones in the group have nothing to say or are detaching themselves. That may or may not be true. In fact, they may be listeners, taking it all in; they may, if asked, surprise you with insight that would have been hard for the most vocal in a group to have gained from the discussion.

A FINAL WORD ON JUDGEMENTS

One day in particular sticks in my mind as a reminder not to judge by appearances. I passed a man on the street at a festival and we smiled at each other. He was scruffy looking, wearing dirty old clothes. Moments later, I was startled to realize that he had turned to follow me and was running to catch up. He said he had to thank me for the beautiful smile that made his day. With that, he made my day, too. Later, I passed a nice looking, well-dressed man and we smiled, then he called out, "Nice knockers!" How's that for a reminder of *don't judge a book by its cover*? This guy must be getting smiles all day long while, for the gentle man I met earlier, smiles were so precious and rare. What a shame.

LISTENERS UNITE!

Imagine a circle of people, a country, a world, where every individual made the careful effort to listen, even just a little bit more. You—as someone who takes listening seriously—make a difference, and increasing numbers of people are taking an interest in researching, learning, teaching, and practicing listening skills.

"Geez! I've never been so nervous giving a speech! I - I can't think when everyone is staring at me!"

In fact, there is an international organization that brings dedicated listeners together. The International Listening Association (ILA) represents 15 countries and 49 states. How do they maintain the feel of a tightly knit community? Says the ILA: "Simple. We listen to each other."

My own website, www.ListenersUnite.com, provides an ongoing blog about listening and has also branched out into an interactive listening group at Groups.Myspace.com/ListenersUnite, where listeners can discuss *virtually* anything about listening.

A CENTURY OF DIALOGUE

Communication is the foundation of successful businesses, relationships, families, and societies. So much suffering, from the most intimate relationships to international relations, is caused or perpetuated by not listening, not having *genuine dialogue*. The Dalai Lama had this to say as we approached the 21st Century: "We can describe this century as a century of bloodshed, a century of war. The next century should be a century of dialogue."

IN SUM

The final frontier may be human
relationships, one person to another.
Buzz Aldrin, Astronaut

We may go in and out of using certain listening skills, lunge forward and fall back, as with anything; however, over time, deepening the practice of placing attention leads to stronger relationships and greater self awareness. By listening—and continually exploring our own listening challenges—we discover ourselves, learn about others, and gain greater knowledge of the world.

Check in on yourself and encourage others to provide you with feedback. If you filled out a self assessment in the beginning of this book and asked others to assess you, go back from time to time to see what may have changed. Even beyond those questions, what have you noticed? Become an observer and listen in on your inner dialogue and your interactions with others. Observe your listening in seminars or meetings.

Every journey begins with one small step. Wherever you are on your listening journey, never lose heart. In the "Listeners Speak" boxes, you may have noticed listening/communication professionals who candidly speak of their own listening challenges. Even the most conscientious listener will have a weakness or two and some just plain off days. But listening is such an integral part of our lives that every skill we practice and incorporate, every time we notice a short circuit or a bit of head static or become more conscious about how and where we place our attention, we are strengthening the foundations for happiness and success in all of the relationships in our lives. By listening, we both show and earn respect and we gain valuable information along the way.

As we learn and grow in our relationships, careers, fields of study, self awareness, and spiritual lives, Rule #1 is *Listen*.

SOURCES

American Heritage Dictionary, 4th ed., Houghton Mifflin, 2000.

American Speech-Language Hearing Association (ASHA), www.asha.org

Beckwith, Harry. *What Clients Love.* New York: Warner Business Books, 2003.

Better Hearing Institute, www.betterhearing.org

Buber, Martin. *Between Man and Man* (2nd edition). London:. Routledge, 2003, (first published in England, 1947).

Collins, Billy. *Nine Horses. New York:* Random House Trade Paperbacks, 2003.

Campbell, Don. *The Mozart Effect.* New York: Harper Paperbacks, 2001.

Down the Rabbit Hole, Captured Light, 2006.

Floyd, James J. *Dialogue versus Monologue: A Listener's Challenge.* a paper presented at the 2006 International Listening Association conference.

Hay, Louise. *Heal Your Body A-Z, The Mental Causes for Physical Illness and the Way to Overcome them. California:* Hay House, 2001.

International Listening Association (ILA), Listen.org

Kennedy, Chris. "Listening Like a Mediator: Skills and Ideas from Conflict Mediators for Our Everyday Lives," a paper presented at the ILA conference 2006.

Kleiner, Kurt. "Venus in Repose." *Scientific American Mind* magazine, (Dec. 2006/Jan. 2007).

Nielsen Media Research, www.nielsenmedia.com

Nhat Hann, Thich. and Dalai Lama IVX, *Wisdom from Peace Is Every Step,* New York: Peter Pauper Press, 2005.

Ornish, Dr. Dean. *Dr. Dean Ornish's Program for Reversing Heart Disease; The Only System Scientifically Proven to Reverse Heart Disease Without Drugs or Surgery.* New York: Ivy Books, 1995.

Rogers, Dr. Sherry A. *Tired or Toxic:A Blueprint for Health.* New York: Prestige Publications,1990.

Ruiz, Miguel. *The Four Agreements, A Practical Guide to Personal Freedom.* California: Amber-Allen Publishing, 1997 & 2001.

Shafir, Rebecca Z. *The Zen of Listening.* Illinois: Quest Books, 2003.

Smell & Taste Treatment Research Foundation in Chicago, IL.

Stahl, Lesley. *Reporting Live.* New York: Simon and Schuster, 1999.

Thank You for Smoking, Fox Searchlight Pictures, 2005.

Walsh, Ed. "Dancing Until Deaf." *Bay Area Reporter,* 2000.

ABOUT THE AUTHOR

LINDA EVE DIAMOND is a freelance writer with nearly fifteen years of experience in the corporate training field. She has written, developed, customized, and conducted training sessions in communication, management skills, and personal development. She currently serves on the executive board of the International Listening Association (ILA).

Diamond is also the creator of www.ListenersUnite.com, a site for listeners, where she shares her extensive library of listening quotes, thoughts on listening and peace, and a *Have You Heard?* blog with interesting features and news related to listening. She also invites listening discussion at www.groups.myspace.com/listenersunite.

BOOKS AUTHORED AND CO-AUTHORED BY LINDA EVE DIAMOND:

- *Team Building that Gets Results,* Sourcebooks, 2007
- *Perfect Phrases for Building Strong Teams,* McGraw-Hill, 2007
- *Perfect Phrases for Motivating and Rewarding Employees,* McGraw-Hill, 2006
- *TABE (Tests of Adult Basic Education) Level A Workbook,* McGraw-Hill, 2007
- *Executive Writing, American Style,* Apocryphile Press, 2007
- *The Human Experience,* ASJA Press, 2007

For more information on the author and her work visit:
www.ListenersUnite.com & **www.LindaEveDiamond.com**

A Message From Happy About®

Thank you for your purchase of this book from Listeners Press™, a division of Happy About®. The book is available online at http://www.listenerspress.com or at other online and physical bookstores.

Please contact us for quantity discounts at sales@happyabout.info.

If you want to be informed by e-mail of upcoming Happy About® and Listeners Press™ books, please e-mail bookupdate@happyabout.info.

Happy About is interested in you if you are an author who would like to submit a non-fiction book proposal or are a corporation that would like to have a book written for you. Please contact us by e-mail at editorial@happyabout.info or by phone (1-408-257-3000).

LaVergne, TN USA
18 November 2009

164528LV00001B/62/A